Drive-Thru Success

Written by Jenny Copeland
Test driven and co-written by Vhairi Slaven

CONTENTS

DEDICATION

From Jenny
This book is dedicated to Rob, Gary, Megan and Aaron without whom I would not have kept going. Thank you all for your unconditional love and belief! Also to my wonderful family and friends who have been important companions and teachers on my journey. Thank you for your understanding, support, love and forgiveness. And finally, to my test driver Vhairi without whom this book would not have been finally constructed, road tested and produced.

From Vhairi
I dedicate this book to my parents who had the patience to wait until I figured out how to be a decent human being. To my sister, who has always been my greatest supporter. To my other families - the Maclachlans/Collins'- especially to my best friend Lisa who has always been there for me no matter what. There are too many loving and supportive friends to mention, so I would like to dedicate this book to everyone who has ever been kind to me, everyone who has listened to me, everyone who has forgiven me, and everyone who has supported me. Thanks to Jenny for our incredibly interesting conversations. Thanks for your belief, support and kindness. Thanks for being a mentor, a creative partner, a dear friend and an amazing opportunity all in one.

From the two of us
We both dedicate this book to everyone who is on this journey called life and have felt lost. To all those who have gone down the wrong road and wondered how they could ever find their way back. To everyone who has experienced anxiety, depression, addiction, melancholy, self-consciousness, doubt, loneliness, judgement, or alienation. It is not easy to share how you feel about these things, but we felt like we had to share them to let you know that most people feel these things - it doesn't make you weak, sensitive, or weird - it makes you human.

Acknowledgements

We would like to say a huge thanks to the following people for their skills, help, advice and support:

To Abbie Bunton for design work as beautiful as you are and a book cover that is as recognisable as a biscuit wrapper.
To Debbie Sutherland at Kano Design for the fabulous website.
To Abi Smith for being suitably pernickety (her words, not ours)
To Kate Macdonald, in a few short weeks you helped us get super organised, introduced us to Dropbox Docs, and are a constant source of belly-laughter.
To May Smith for your excellent skills with a red pen and your unwavering support.
To Susan Hunter for your honest feedback, encouragement and support.
To John Wilkings for your help, advice and proof-reading skills.
To all of our lovely EVA ladies, thank you for being a source of inspiration and encouragement.
To all of our advanced readers, thank you so much for your valuable feedback.

Jenny's Preface

I wanted to write a book that would enable me to share the simplest process in the world to creating a fulfilling and happy life. I feel fulfilled in life because I am clear about my vision and I have found the time to take the necessary actions to see my dreams come true, this book being one of them.

Drive-Thru Success represents the latest school of thought in the field of coaching, positive psychology, personal success and manifestation. It is the result of 30 years of coaching hundreds of people in a variety of ways: one-to-one, in groups, privately, corporately and in the community.

For 30 years I have studied and obtained a range of qualifications in the following philosophies:
- performance psychology;
- coaching;
- Neuro Linguistic Programming (NLP);
- success psychology and the Law of Attraction with Bob Proctor (featured contributor to *the Secret* by Rhonda Byrne); and
- meta physics (but don't let that put you off) which has enabled me to understand not only the *how* of achievement, but also the *why*.

I have done the reading, experimentation and distillation of information on your behalf and from that have created a refined, effective process that you can follow with confidence. Knowing that by doing so, you will get the results you want, fast. The personal development industry has been growing steadily for the past 100 years and since the late 90s coaching has been recognised as a profession in its own right. Coaching as a discipline is primarily future focused. It challenges you on the basis of what you need to do differently for things to be better or for you to have the things you want that you don't yet have.

Coaching as a discipline is not counselling however it is worthwhile acknowledging that many of the barriers to success are beliefs, behaviours and habits that have been laid down in the past. Coaching does seek to eliminate or address these behaviours in order for the client to be free to behave in a way that will allow them to be, do or have what they want. Before we begin to share our exciting journey of discovery you probably want to know:

Who am I? And what qualifies me to be able to tell you about being successful?

I am a Performance Improvement Coach who for the last 30 years has been providing leadership and organisational development solutions, enabling performance improvement, and delivering organisational success for large and small businesses, both public and private sectors, and more recently for the NHS .

For individuals, I run a successful performance improvement company, **Secrets of Success**. I help executives, and everybody from eight-year-old children to 80-year-old children (at heart anyway) get more from their by lives by creating a life of happiness and fulfilment.

Today, I am a mother to three wonderful children and a wife to a wonderful man. As well as coaching (both voluntary and paid) I work out, practice yoga, attend a visualisation group and continue to expand my knowledge in the field of personal development so that I can be a more effective person, coach and author.

My cup really does runneth over, but it hasn't always been like this.

I was born in London, the daughter of two relatively under-educated Irish runaways. Life was tough and we were poor. I left school with only a handful of O Levels, but I have achieved success in business through hard work and determination. I have been married twice and I was a single parent for 6 years. I have experienced debt, ill health, alcoholism in loved ones, failure, and success.

I started what I call my 'formal education' at 40, and since then I continue to absorb every drop of joy out of life. However, I, like you, am a human being living each day as it comes, dealing with daily challenges and looking out for opportunities. I am real and vulnerable, but hopeful - always endeavouring to live my life to its fullest capacity.

My challenge here is how do I get to share my secrets with you, the reader, in the limited time I have available?

Recognising that most of you don't have the time to devote to long, drawn-out publications, I have decided to keep this book as concise, simple and practical as possible. Therefore this book is designed to be an interactive workbook in which I have used and adapted exercises from some of the best personal development programmes and philosophies in the world. Completed in the order that they have been organised, they will give you the very best and the fastest results.

But you don't need to take my word for it! By way of a living endorsement I have joined forces with my co-driver, Vhairi Slaven. Vhairi has joined me and has test-driven all of the exercises, kindly sharing her thoughts and experiences along the way. She has not held back and I hope by observing her journey you can see how you too can benefit from **Drive-Thru Success** even when you are not totally sure about your own understanding.

I promised you short and sharp, so let's get on with it! I would like to formally introduce you to Vhairi, my test-driver ...

Vhairi's Preface

Before I knew anything about energy I went along with things with no real sense of direction, no goals, and no beliefs. I thought for a time that meaning in life could come from love and didn't at the time understand that when people talk about love being 'all you need' and such, they are not talking about romantic love, but a different kind. I realised that being loved by a man was not only not enough, but that it actually accentuated all of the feelings of depression, unworthiness and hopelessness that I was experiencing.

I realised that I couldn't continue in life without believing in something. I had to search for something or I was going to self-destruct completely. I cared too much for the people in my life to do that. So during that time, unconsciously, in my darker moments, I begged to some higher power, whatever it might be, to show me what my purpose was. Irrespective of how rational or not it is to believe in a higher power, I was very aware that it was important for me if I wanted to do anything except suffer. I see now that this was in fact my first experience of ASK.

In my twenties, I met an older couple, Dot and Laurie, who had done something called the Silva Course which was very popular in the 80s. They continually talked about energy and 'asking the angels'. I thought they were very eccentric, but articulate, intelligent and interested in talking about life. I felt liberated finding people willing to talk to me about these things. My family and friends always made comments about me being too deep, but here I was sitting in my office in a picturesque village in the country speaking to a 70-year old man about the fact that everything was made of energy and that it came from some kind of power that we did not fully understand.

Dot gave me a book by Louise Hay called *Affirmations to Heal Your Life*. When I first read it to myself, I cried. I had never talked to myself in such a loving, forgiving, positive way. It made me realise how cruel I had been to myself. I read many other books looking for answers - about religions, philosophies, and life experiences. Finally a book called *Joyful Wisdom* by Yongey Mingyur Rinpoche changed the way I thought about everything. It explained meditation and mindfulness in a simple, reasonable and practical way. I read several other books about Buddhism, and decided that I liked the way they thought about things.

At the age of 28, I decided to learn to drive. It was the first big thing I had tried to achieve in years. It took me eight attempts to pass, and in order to calm my nerves I tried out what I had been reading about in the books: meditating (not medicating as my dad thought when I told him). It calmed me in a way nothing ever had before. I became more open to different ways of looking at things and I found an understanding of life that I knew would never be confirmed, that sounded irrational, but that I believed in anyway. I had found faith, and it felt like I might finally be able to pull myself out of the slump that I was in.

I was still not on the right path, however. The stress and unhappiness with the work I was doing encouraged me to make the decision to go to Australia. Had I not been introduced to this kind of thought, I would never have believed I could get there, I would not have had the motivation to save, or the balls to go on my own. I travelled for two years and the experience changed the way I saw everything around me. I also started writing again, something I had last done when I was around ten years old.

When I came home I poured into words everything I was thinking and feeling, everything I had learned and now understood about life, and I realised that this was my medicine. I also realised that it was something that I could work hard at and that could give me the opportunity to make a living doing something I love and to travel more. I decided to make it my vision to be a paid writer.

I read a book called *Grace* by Christine McGrory. It explained all of the self-development ideas and practices that I was becoming drawn to in a simple, reasonable and graceful way. It inspired me to create a vision board. I started writing down what it was I wanted out of life. I wrote it in lists, I wrote stories about it, and I drew it in a picture. I did *The Key*® weekend course with the author of *Grace*, it explained the science of energy in a way I could easily understand and gave me a greater understanding of the kinds of things I could do to believe I deserve the things I want to achieve.

I read Jack Canfield's *Principles of Success* and did the exercises in it. Again I wrote down the things that I wanted the most. One of the things I wrote down was that I wanted a mentor and to find more people who I could talk to about the things I was really interested in. I wanted to get paid to write.

Slowly, but surely, I am getting the things I ASK for - working on this book with Jenny is one of them.

My visions are now lofty, and I have a fair distance to go in my learning and development, but I have to acknowledge how far I have come. I feel like I belong here on this earth, and that I am worthy of being happy. I am no longer nervous and self-conscious. I can walk into a room with my head held high, completely sober. I can honestly say that I am completely comfortable in my own skin. I sincerely want everyone to feel the same, which is why I have decided to share my journey with you as I test-drive Drive-Thru Success.

Invitation to Drive Straight Thru

Welcome to your simple instruction manual on how to be successful.

This book is designed to be an interactive workbook. You may prefer to read it in full and then reread it and do the exercises, or to read it and complete the exercises as you go, either way will work.

The exercises can be found at http://drive-thrusuccess.com/exercises/ and you can interact with us and our other test-drivers at @drivethrusuccess on Facebook. To receive exclusive access to the exercises, the DTS Facebook Group and our mailing list, buy this book and go to the back where you will find instructions.

It was when working with youth groups that I began to use the metaphor for the **3 simple steps that** brought them to life in a truly simplistic way. I would ask them to imagine that they were visiting a drive-thru restaurant or burger bar. Those of you that have been through a drive-thru will know (and if you don't, it is a very simple process to understand), that in a drive-thru restaurant there are three simple steps to receiving your meal. This book will show you that in life there are also three simple steps to creating the life you want and to manifest your dreams or desires on a day-to-day basis.

The 3 simple steps in Drive-Thru Success

Step 1: ASK – place your order
Step 2: ACT – pay for your order
Step 3: ACTUALISE – pick up your order

You will also know that it is a well-oiled, highly systematic process. Its essence is its simplicity. I shall be referring to this metaphor throughout, as it is central to our process of achieving success.

Like my own **3 simple steps in Drive-Thru Success**, fast food drive-thrus tend to work every time. Have you ever gone into the kitchen to check that everything is being prepared as per your request? No, we trust that the cook or Chef has understood our order and has all the ingredients and equipment to fulfil it. Personal success works in exactly the same way. There is a 'cook' working on our behalf. Unseen to us, she or he listens to our every request and always cooks up a formula to meet our demands.

I keep repeating that these steps are very simple, and they are. However there is a health warning attached to them - **we cannot <u>not</u> follow them**. What this means is that we are in fact now (yes, you and me and each and every human being on the planet) currently following these steps.

The problem is that a shockingly high percentage of the world population is not aware of the fact that they are following the steps already. Even those that are aware of them are either not conscious that they are using them, or they are not aware how to use them on a day-to-day basis. My experience is that this is the case for 98% of my client's. In other words, we are either already clear about what we want in a positive way and are in the process of manifestation, or we are oblivious to the fact that we are actively accepting the status quo, or that our 'giving up on life' attitude is giving us the results we experience in life now.

Bob Proctor, a personal success guru and contributor to the book *The Secret* repeats over and over in his work: 'If you want to know what a person is thinking … look at their results.'

Following the **3 simple steps in Drive-Thru Success** allows you to consciously engage in the process of creating your own future. It allows you be clear about what it is you are asking for, take responsibility for acknowledging the action required to take you towards your dreams, and to be able to recognise opportunities and the dreams themselves when they do show up.

Then when your desires do show up - and trust me, they will – it allows you to reach out and grab them with both hands safe in the knowledge you have helped to create them. Some people will of course call this LUCK. I call it **Drive-Thru Success** and enjoy experiencing the results of following the steps every day.
If, like me, you are a highly experiential learner there is nothing stopping you from jumping into your metaphorical car and using the **3 simple steps in Drive-Thru Success** straight way!

Step 1:   ASK - place your order
State your desire loud and clear.

Simply decide what you want and either say clearly or write it on a piece of paper. Don't censor yourself or edit your desire.

Step 2:   ACT - pay for your order
Action is the currency of success.

Either think of or jot down on a piece of paper all the things you could do and start doing what you can, little or large, straight away.

Step 3:   ACTUALISE – pick up your order
Grab opportunities with both hands.

Now be aware of and start to notice the thing(s) you have asked for turning up, or the opportunities that will take you closer to it. You may be blown away by the speed at which it shows up! As I always say to my clients, 'Hold onto your hat!' This quick start method will certainly get you going, however there are many reasons why you don't magically manifest. You can get in your own way, you can sabotage your own success, and you can simply be blind to seeing that you have manifested and walk straight past it.

It is possible that the reason behind many of these scenarios is because of your vibration. You will also learn how your own state of vibration impacts on your ability to accelerate or decelerate your progress. You will discover how to maximise and manage your vibrational energy to help you supercharge your manifestation abilities.

In addition to **the 3 simple steps in Drive-Thru Success** I have selected **20 Secrets of Success** to increase your understanding and development to allow you to improve and maintain a positive vibration. Within these secrets are the beliefs and habits that if embraced and practiced will provide you with an approach to life that will underpin and support your successful life.

As with many aspects of life, you will get out of this book what you put in. Your success destination will only be reached with continuous use of the success principles. This book provides you with all you need to start your visionary journey, but if you want to experience success day by day, make sure you apply the principles in your life every day as often as you can.

The final deed in the whole process is to take time to celebrate your wins, manifestations or achievements, call them what you will. Taking time to recognise that you have participated in the manifestation, and to be grateful for your ability to make good things happen in your life, reconnects you to your part in the process and reminds you to use the process more.

Reading the book and doing the exercises will help deepen your understanding of the manifestation process and help you be in the very best condition to create the wonderful life you desire.

'Begin doing what you want to do now. We are not living in eternity. We have only this moment, sparkling like a star in our hand and melting like a snowflake.'

Sir Francis Bacon Sr.

SECRETS OF SUCCESS 1: BEING SUCCESSFUL IS EASY

Success is available to everybody.

In the same way that gravity keeps every single person rooted to the earth, it doesn't decide to keep certain people standing because they are lucky, rich, beautiful or smart, whilst letting others fall into space. It works for each and every one of us. The same simple laws of the Universe govern success. That's right, there are more laws of nature than the ones we are taught about at school or university. For many people they remain a mystery their whole lives and sadly they live and die unaware that their lives could have been enriched by simply following some of these laws. Imagine what would happen if we knew about, understood, and followed ALL of them.

Equally, these laws do not sit idle because we are not fully conscious of them. We do not float around the atmosphere unaffected by them until eventually we learn about gravity and then, hey presto, we come down to earth with a bump!

In fact there are many people who are successful but unaware of the fact that they are following any 'laws' as such. These people will either have developed their own set of rules, or have been nurtured in an environment where the laws are followed naturally. In training we call it unconscious competence.

If you are one of these people you may find yourself acknowledging your awareness that many of these **Secrets of Success** sound familiar or are principles or philosophies you already follow. If so, that's great, this book will be a reinforcement of what you are already doing and it may help you appreciate more what you have or you may find that by following the exercises you can supercharge or accelerate your success to the next level.

The clients I work with tend to fall into a range of camps:
- Successful and looking to move to the next level.
- Working towards a goal but not making the progress desired.
- At a crossroads and unsure what to do next.
- Unhappy or stuck, and looking for a way to improve the quality of their lives.

Regardless of why clients come to me, developing an understanding of and working with all of the success principles outlined in this book allows them to achieve the level of success they desire in their lives. You too can experience success and happiness. All you have to do is follow the instructions in this book:

- Learn the **20 Secrets of Success.**
- Complete the exercises.
- Develop successful habits.
- Follow the **3 simple steps in Drive-Thru Success.**

WARNING: Following all of the principles of success could seriously change your life for the better!

Over the many years I have worked with people, I have witnessed wonderful examples of success, not least of all in my own life. Throughout the book I will share with you actual accounts of how people have managed to create the lives they choose using these principles, and of course Vhairi is also sharing her first journey using **Drive-Thru Success.** She is sharing with you her exercises, plus an account of how her life changes as she practices the secrets and follows the steps.

Most of the people I work with have no prior knowledge of the **Drive-Thru Success** or the **20 Secrets of Success** yet once they follow the steps they consistently experience success and happiness. My client, we'll call her Josie, had reached a crossroads in her career and was considering what to do next. Josie followed the process I shall describe to you and created a compelling vision of her future. She could see herself working abroad, expanding her skills and gaining international experience. She set herself a two-year time frame for her goal and used a visualisation of herself going through the international departure gate at the airport feeling confident and happy, carrying Louis Vuitton luggage.

Within 9 months she had been offered a job in Dublin and was on her way. She subsequently worked in Spain and Holland before finally deciding she wanted to return to the UK. A week after we created her 'return to the UK' plan she 'bumped into' a mutual colleague who was in a position to offer her an ideal role based in the UK.

Now you may say this is all sheer coincidence and there was a time that I would have agreed with you. However, I have documented too many of these cases to write them off as random events. I know these synchronicities are the results of a combination of forces all working together, one of which is the action taken by clients that facilitates these wonderful realisations of dreams. I prefer to think about the outcomes as co-ordinated incidents!

EVERYBODY AND ANYBODY CAN BE SUCCESSFUL - MOST OF US ARE EVEN IF WE DON'T KNOW IT!

In order to develop **Secrets of Success 1** we need to examine what we mean by success. Defining what success means to you is the starting point from which we will work together to create it.

What I have learned about success:

- Success is a very personal thing.
- Success can mean different things to different people.
- Success can mean the attainment of a goal.
- Success can mean the pursuit of a goal.
- Success can mean a feeling of happiness.
- Success can mean a sense of calm or peace of mind.
- Success can mean winning.
- Success can mean taking part.
- Success can mean re-evaluating where you are and what you have and deciding that it is your best choice.
- Success can mean passing exams or studying for pleasure.
- Success can mean being rich or being happy living within your means.
- Success can mean driving a fast car or choosing to walk to help save our planet.
- Success can mean living in a big house with a large mortgage or living on a smallholding and owning it completely.

- Success can mean travelling around the world or enjoying a week in a campsite.
- Success can mean having a great job or indeed any job at all.

Success can have many meanings. Too many people are measuring their own success using somebody else's success criteria. Like looking into a mirror and expecting to see another person's reflection or putting on someone else's clothes and wondering why they are so loose or tight and don't look as good on you.

We can admire the attributes in others, we can aspire to be like them however we need to be true to ourselves and recognise our own unique hopes and aspirations. It is these very ideas that become our personal vision and help define our own success criteria.

Exercise 1: Defining Success

An important first step in creating your success criteria (which will eventually evolve into your personal vision) is to consider what success means for you. Take some time to think about the following questions and make some notes. Use a separate piece of paper if you need more space or go to www.drive-thrusuccess.com/exercises/ to download the exercises.

1.	What does success mean to you?
2.	What will be happening in your life when you are successful or more successful than you are now?
3.	How will you be thinking, feeling, and what will you be saying?
4.	How will you look?
5.	What will you be wearing?
6.	Who is with you in this picture?

Whatever you have written is the first step towards you crafting a wonderful future for yourself. You will have the opportunity further on to refine and clarify your personal vision, but for now being truthful with yourself as to what success will mean to you is a positive first step.

I think it is fair to say that true success is a state of mind. It is so personal that only you can decide for yourself what will make you feel successful. And in there lies another point: **how will you feel when you know you have been successful?**

Modern living is running at such a pace that it is far too easy to become achievement junkies. No sooner has one goal been attained and we are off chasing the next. Now I am not saying that being goal-centric is a bad thing, but it is important to take time to stop and recognise our achievements and to take time to **CELEBRATE** them.

Often when people are asked to talk about the aspects of themselves that they like, they struggle. When asked to talk about the aspects of themselves that they would like to change, they are quick to reel off a list as long as their arm.

Exercise 2: Celebrate yourself

Think about the headings and write down as many things as come to mind under each heading. You may need to use a separate piece of paper or you can download the form from the website.

Things I like about myself	Things I don't like about myself
Things I am proud of	Things I wish I could change
Some of my achievements	Things I wish I could complete

This is a simple test to give a sense of how well developed or resilient your self-esteem is. As you can imagine, a long list of positives will indicate a positive self-esteem, whilst a long list of negatives will indicate that a person has a negative or less favourable self-esteem. Think about the list as credits and debits in your self-esteem bank account. You may also consider them as oil in your engine. A strong self-esteem (a full engine) will run smoothly and take you to your destination efficiently and economically. A weak self-esteem (low oil) will make the journey harder and at worst seize the engine completely, meaning you aren't going anywhere!

Recognising and taking time to celebrate our successes allows us to register and record that we have achieved something.

When we do this we learn to identify what it feels like to be successful so that even when we achieve a small, seemingly insignificant success, we benefit from recognising the positive emotions we feel and take the time to deposit the 'win' in our self-esteem bank account. The more deposits we have in our self-esteem bank account, the more money we have to spend at the drive-thru. Improved self-esteem will result in increased sense of well being and happiness, more energy and confidence, and less second-guessing and hesitation. The better we feel about ourselves the more positive and hopeful we are about the future.

This upward cycle of positivity is very important because how we feel about 'things' affects how we think about them. It is a combination of our thoughts and feelings that creates our focus - positive or negative. A lot has been written over the years about Positive Mental Attitude or PMA, but thinking positively in isolation without any other form of action will probably not amount to much. However, thinking negatively or looking on the downside will certainly harm your prospects of achieving anything.

So for now, congratulate yourself that you have initiated the manifestation process by starting to define your own success criteria to become clearer as to how you want your life to be in the future.

Although your success journey will most likely involve other people along the way, the most important traveller is you. Being clear about who you see yourself to be is fundamental to your success, and the next chapter **Secrets of Success 2: I AM WHO I SEE MYSELF TO BE** will take you further on that journey by teaching you how to develop the best version of yourself. Before we go to this chapter let's hear from Vhairi and see how she got along with the first the exercises.

Test Drive I

For years, I did not believe success was easy. I believed that only certain people could be successful, and that they were born with gifts and personalities that I did not have and would never have. When I was very young I wanted to be an actress and although I did go to a drama class in primary school, ultimately I gave up on that dream because I believed that I was not attractive enough and that I was born in a place and in social circumstances that meant it was not possible for me. I also thought that talent was something you either had or you didn't, and that I didn't have it. I felt at the time that I didn't have the support of my family or indeed anyone. I realise now that the only thing that stopped me was a lack of belief in myself. Had I been determined, I would have found people around me (family, friends or otherwise) who would have supported me and I would have found a way.

I held the belief that success was for other people until my late twenties. I was, however, quite intelligent and managed to get good grades at school despite being a very disillusioned and unhappy young girl.

I left school and instead of going straight to University, got a job in a call centre in Glasgow. I realised then that I did actually want to pursue some kind of career in film, and went to college to study communications and media and then University to study cinema and cultural studies. I did well at both, yet when the time came to apply for jobs in the media, I still held on to the same negative beliefs about myself. I thought that all of the jobs were in London and there were so many people who had more talent and more charisma than me, that it was impossible for me to get a job in that field. I fell into jobs and even enjoyed them to an extent, but I was aware that I was not doing what I should be doing. I still believed that success was meant for people other than me.

It wasn't until I began to learn about energy and the law of attraction that I thought that maybe success was not something you were, but something you did, and that I was capable of learning how to do it. I knew that I didn't know enough and that I needed a mentor, so I asked for one, and in one very synchronistic week I received two unexpected coaching sessions, one of which was with Jenny.

Not only did the Universe present me with a mentor, it presented me with the opportunity to work through a structured set of success principles and exercises while writing a book. I have to say, that the way that opportunity came up and was presented to me gave me butterflies and made my face turn red. Imagine telling someone you barely know that you want to be a writer for the first time and them replying, "Well that's interesting, I have had a book sitting in a drawer for years and I have been looking for someone to help me finish it. Why don't you test drive the book and I will mentor you as you do it?" I am not even joking about how that whole afternoon went.

I was making these things happen in my life. I was accepting responsibility for the frequency my energy was vibrating at and when I used that energy while working on achieving my goals, the opportunities to achieve them just seemed to come out of nowhere. Of course they didn't – I was attracting them.

Of course I have to be clear about what my goals are. So let me test drive the first lot of exercises for you to give you an idea of where to start when thinking about your own goals.

Test drive exercise 1: Defining yourself-

1. What does success mean to you?
I am doing creative work that I love, that inspires people and that allows me to travel freely and have a permanent base in Scotland.

2. What will be happening in your life when you are successful or more successful than you are now?
I am living a varied life. I am in touch with a lot of like-minded people. I have lots of projects on the go.

3. How will you be thinking, feeling, and what will you be saying?
I feel inspired, motivated and energetic. I am vibrating on an energy that is magnetic to other people. I am proud and happy with myself. I am constantly amazed by all of the wonderful things that are happening in my life.

4. How will you look?
I look glowing. I have healthy skin, hair and teeth. I am physically fit and slim. I have a unique style. I am confident in my own skin.

5. What will you be wearing?
I am wearing funky, trendy clothes. I look clean and smart, but edgy. I am colourful. I have time to shop in lots of great vintage stores and find unusual things that other people wouldn't wear.

6. Who is with you in this picture?
My family, Abbie, Lisa and their families, my partner, and Jenny. We are celebrating our success. My parents are there, huge smiles on their faces. I have a big group of friends and supporters from all of the jobs I have had, and from all the groups I go to and through current projects.

Test drive exercise 2: Celebrate yourself

Things I like about myself	Things I don't like about myself
• I embrace my weirdness. • I am brave. • I am compassionate. • I have a big heart. • I am someone who champions other people. • I question everything. • I am aware. • I am open to new ideas. • I have my own style. • I am curious. • I am fun. • I am silly. • I like people. • I always finish the things I have started. • I always try to do what I say I will do. • I have integrity. • I have passion. • I am honest. • I am humble. • I am non-judgemental. • I don't care about social perceptions of me. • I am open to feedback and eager to learn.	• I can be self-conscious. • I can be defensive. • I don't take criticism well. • I can be too hard on myself. • I can let negative people affect my own energy. • I doubt my talent and my intelligence sometimes. • I get anxious. • I doubt myself and the things I know. • I get bored easily.

Things I am proud of	Things I wish I could change
• The way I have forgiven everyone who has hurt me. • The way I have taught myself to be strong even though I am so sensitive. • The fact that I have the courage to dream big and to dare. • How far I have come in terms of confidence, self-belief, fitness, the way I look, and my career. • My sister and how far she has come.	• Stop caring about whether people think my beliefs are stupid or crazy. • I would like to be kinder to myself. • I would like to be more daring. • I would like to stop doubting whether I am doing the right things with my life. • I wish I could help my sister feel more confident. • I wish everyone I love could be happy. • I wish I had money to help the people around me.
Things I have achieved	**Things I want to finish**
• Getting a short story published. • Sharing my writing . • Creating my own website. • Running a half-marathon. • Getting to a size 8/10 and a 26 inch waist. • Doing a headstand. • Getting movie reviews published. • Getting a university degree. • Getting a Communications job. • Going to Australia on my own. • Sky-diving. • Becoming a yoga teacher.	• Drive-Thru Success. • Miss Jane (a novel). • Getting paid for a movie review in a published magazine or newspaper. • In my Communications job – the website.

'Personal success is knowing that I have done my best and I am enough.'
- Jenny Copeland

Secrets of Success 2: I AM WHO I SEE MYSELF TO BE

Remember it is up to you to define what success really means to you. Having drafted your first idea of success you may already be re-thinking your original version. That's ok. You will be writing your exciting personal vision later in the workbook. By taking the time to read this book and complete the exercises you are already a success in my eyes!

You will be deciding what your own goals are and you will decide your own success criteria. It may be helpful to think of success in these three ways:

- **Success at Being someone**
- **Success at Doing something**
- **Success at Having something**

Exercise 3: Success at Being Someone

Living consciously from our own values enriches our lives and allows us to really get the most from our time. If you have never done a values exercise here's your chance to have a go. If you have, why not do the exercise anyway and see if your values have realigned.

If you were to look in the mirror you would see yourself (unless of course, you are a vampire). Presumably you have a name for yourself and you would be able to describe who you are. But are you seeing all of you? Access this exercise at www.drive-thrusuccess.com/exercises

---

1. If I were to ask you how successful are you as an individual, what rating would you give yourself out of 10?

0 is useless and 10 is fabulous. Mark your score along this line:

0	5	10

---

2. Have a look at this list of roles and responsibilities that apply to many people in life. Now tick √ each box that applies to you.			
Son		Wife	
Daughter		Boyfriend	
Brother		Colleague	
Sister		Grandson	
Friend		Granddaughter	
Cousin		Auntie	
Employee		Uncle	
Boss		Girlfriend	
Nephew		Student	
Niece		Teacher	
Husband		In-law	
Other		Other	

You have probably ticked at the very least two boxes and many of you will have ticked many more. Feel free to define additional relationships in the other boxes or change the wording as you see fit. I have two brothers so I have two brother boxes as my relationship with each brother is different.

Use the following scoring lines to plot a success score for each relationship you have marked above. Mark your rating out of 10 as to how successful you think you are at each role. 10 is the highest score. You can download these charts from www.drive-thrusuccess.com/exercises.

Role:

0	5	10

I will presume that you marked yourself differently from one relationship to another. Go back and have a look at how you scored yourself as an individual. We can all be experiencing varying degrees of success in different areas of our life. The challenge is how to be balanced and realistic regarding how we feel about ourselves in relation to the scores. For example if you have had an argument or estrangement from a parent, and you really don't feel good about it, you may consciously or unconsciously allow your 'failure' at that one relationship to overshadow your many other successful relationships.

It's important to think about how deeply some relationships can affect your overall happiness. You may score yourself as a 10 in your marriage, as a parent yourself, or with your friends, but a poor relationship with a parent can affect you so much unconsciously that you score your own current happiness as a 4 without being aware of why you are feeling so low! This is why putting the time and effort into thinking about each aspect of who you are being is so important.

Success at Being Someone

It is sometimes useful to ask the people you are in a relationship with how they rate how you for this exercise. This is what is known as 360° feedback. As you can imagine this is not the easiest thing to do, but if people understand you want honest feedback in order for you to improve how you behave, then they may welcome the opportunity to give you the feedback. Maybe it will be an opportunity to tell you how great you are or maybe it will be a chance to at last tell you a few home truths. Either way you have to be prepared to brace yourself, grit your teeth, keep a smile on your face and say: 'Thank you for that feedback, I will take it into consideration.' I believe that **There's no such thing as criticism only feedback!** which you will come to in **Secrets of Success number 10**) Feedback that helps us develop is the greatest gift of all.

I will share with you my current assessment of how I rate in my **Success at Being Someone** chart at the moment.

Mother	0		✪	7/10
Daughter	0		✪	10/10
Boss	0		✪	8/10
Coach	0		✪	9/10
Supplier	0		✪	9/10
Friend (B list)	0		✪	8/10
Sister to John	0		✪	9/10
Sister to Tommy	0		✪	7/10
Aunty	0		✪	9/10
Niece	0		✪	8/10
Volunteer	0	✪		5/10
Friend (C list)	0	✪		5/10

Now I don't know about you, but I find this interesting viewing for two reasons. Firstly the order in which I have placed the items, and secondly that I rate higher in less important relationships than the most important ones: my husband and children. I will draw your attention to the fact that my deceased parents are on my values list. This is because, although they are no longer physically here with me, I still choose to have responsibilities and duties to them or on their behalf that I consider important, for example maintaining contact with their brothers and sisters and maintaining their graves. This is not so easy as my mother's grave is abroad, but I do my best with my father's.

I am always very careful to ensure these duties are done with a willing heart and I derive immense pleasure from still being able to do things for my parents. I have also had the pleasure of forming some of the most important and special relationships in my life with my aunts, uncles and cousins.

You will also notice that I have Friends B List and C list but no A list. I will explore this in greater detail, in **Success Number 9: YOU CAN'T PLEASE ALL OF THE PEOPLE ALL OF THE TIME.** However, just for now, embrace the concept that the only people to make your A list will be the people with whom you have the very closest relationships, for example, the people you would consider your 'significant other' or closest 'family', who may of course be friends.

Let's look at these aspects individually and then it will be your turn to have another go.

Energy Vampires

Have you ever noticed how we can end up giving a lot of our time and energy to the kind of people I would call energy vampires? In the past I had friends who only ever called me when there was a disaster. They would interrupt my day and launch into a tirade about their problems, asking me for my opinion. Now, I am not saying I didn't enjoy this. In many ways it fed my own need to be needed and I happily allowed this to continue for years. Also, if I am honest I think I also played this behaviour out myself and in the end I had created a nice little co-dependent group of angst junkies. A co-dependent relationship is one where one person (or in this case a group of people) supports or enables another's addiction, poor mental health, or destructive behaviour.

One particular aspect of this process that eventually became wearing was that we never really followed each other's advice. Once we had exhausted the ear of one friend we would go onto the next regaling the same sorry story of how we had been wronged, or why we were unhappy being so fat, in debt, or single.

Friend number two would also offer his or her version of advice, which often was contrary to the first friend's and so the merry-go-round would continue.
As by way of an introduction to the **Secret Of Success 3: WHAT YOU PUT YOUR FOCUS ON IS WHAT YOU GET**, what were we doing? We were focusing on what was wrong. Stuck in the misery of the event or circumstance for hours or days, even weeks, months or years. Energetically we were immersed in negative energy. By continually harping on about our woes, we were not only guaranteeing that we stayed in that frame of mind, we were increasing the likelihood that we would never change our situation.

One day I woke up to my co-dependency habit with help from my very special friend Deborah who explained two very clever things. The first was her observation that I seemed to spend lots of my time with people with problems or issues. Was that not fairly easy seeing as most people have problems or issues, I thought?

Secondly, and most importantly, she told me that she would only ever listen to a problem of mine once. She would offer advice and then assume I would do something. If I didn't do anything, and my 'problem' resurfaced in conversation, she would kindly point out that we had already covered this ground and because nothing has changed, neither had her opinion!
Deborah had something I didn't. She had self-esteem and self-worth. She had a clear idea of how she wanted to spend her time and what would make her feel good. This is not to say that she isn't the most wonderful friend a girl could have but she wasn't prepared to be my crutch. True friendship to her is providing a supportive ear, offering sound advice and then moving on to being cheerful.

What if we can't solve the problem or a plan doesn't work?
Where topics are outside our range of capability we can research and find a specialist who can help. The list of specialists available to us these days is fairly exhaustive. I have personally tried or used most of them, and in some situations, I have used more than one before I have found the one best suited to the situation.

Tony Robbins poses a useful question, which is relevant when resolving issues or problems: 'What do you do if something doesn't work?'

The simple answer is to try a different approach. If that doesn't work, try another different approach and keep trying until you either resolve the issue or problem, accept that it isn't such a big deal after all and that you can live with it. Some situations, illnesses, or natural disasters may mean that acceptance of the situation is what is required. This will lead to a gentle vibration that allows you to be open to strategies that help you make the best of the situation.

Remember:

'For every ailment under the sun
There is a remedy, or there is none;
If there is one, try to find it;
If there is none, never mind it.'
-Friedrich Schiller

Here are some specialists that I have used in the past:

- GP
- Medical specialist / consultant
- Midwife
- Chiropractor
- Counsellor
- Therapist
- Hypnotherapist
- Lawyer / solicitor
- Bank manager
- Financial advisor
- Chiropodist
- Homeopath
- The internet
- Reflexologist
- Coach
- Friend

The impact of my co-dependent behaviour was that people who were not necessarily close or valuable to me were managing to eat into my available time. This left me poor of time for my most important relationships.

My most important relationships were with my husband and children, however due to the way I was prioritising my time, they wouldn't have known that. Prior to doing this exercise my husband and children ranked below my job and were on an equal par to some of my 'best friends'.

I decided to make my husband and children my top priority - above all else. This has subsequently made saying no to non-important invitations and requests for demands on my time so much easier. Over the years I have developed the ability to say no without feeling like I have to justify why I am saying no. Now that is what I call freedom and as a by-product, I am able to confidently say that my family know that they are my top priority.

Bearing this in mind, have another look at your own relationship lists and prioritisation. You may want to change the order of priority yourself. Once you have established your base score you can then go about deciding what score you would like that relationship to have.

Success at Doing Something

As we have already discussed, we are all currently enjoying success doing lots of different things. If I were to ask you how many things you are currently being successful at, you would probably answer between 0 and 50, depending on what you do and how you spend your time.
People who are in employment or education often have external measurements for their success. They may have work reviews, exams or essays to measure themselves against. It is important not to fall into the trap of using someone else's assessment of success to totally define yourself.

I recently completed a development course and my measure of success was to achieve a practical competence at the intervention. The trainer wanted me to write an academic piece that would secure me a top rate pass. I did not consider the time it would take to write the piece to her standard important, and was happy to write a price that proved my underpinning knowledge to a satisfactory level, securing me a pass mark.

It was clear that my measure of success and her expectation of my goal were different. Not everybody, every time wants to be outstanding. What we are capable of is setting our own clear criteria of success and doing what is required to achieve that. That is more important and more fulfilling than trying to achieve someone else's expectations of success.

Other people who are not seen to be in full-time or part-time employment or education may not have such clear-cut success criteria to work to. Many stay-at-home mothers or pensioners, when asked this question, answer zero. Whether you are in work or out of work, as a student, a mother or a father, whether you are retired or semi-retired, you are already doing many things successfully every day. Let's consider what you are currently doing successfully:

- Getting out of bed.
- Brushing your teeth.
- Getting dressed.
- Reading and writing.
- Cooking or reheating meals.
- Preparing wholesome meals that sustain life.
- Managing a household budget (often creatively).
- Assisting new human beings to be functional.
- Assisting new human beings to be successful themselves.
- Communicating.
- Negotiating.
- Planning.

We really do underestimate how complex some of these tasks are. Firstly we had to learn to do the actions and then we have to motivate ourselves to keep on doing them day in and day out. We could choose not to start some of these activities, which would result in us neglecting ourselves. So if you are managing to complete them each day in a relatively orderly fashion, I congratulate you at being successful at 'doing' living.

Success at Having Something

So as we become clearer and more responsible for who we are being and what we are doing, we can also start thinking about setting goals and making lists about what we want to have in our lives.

The same philosophy of success criteria applies to having as it does to doing and being. We set our own criteria. What we need to be careful about is that it is that we are sure that it is in fact our own self-defined desires that we are going after and not the wants or not wants of our parents, friends or indeed society.

What beliefs are we attaching to our desires to 'have'?
I grew up in relative poverty; however as a young teenager I can remember watching both Coronation Street and Dallas. As I watched both of these programmes, I was drawn to and aspired to have the lifestyle that I observed while watching Dallas. I daydreamed about driving an open-top car - I didn't even know then that they were called cabriolets. I visualised a ranch with a swimming pool, my own business and me kitted out in the clothes Pam and Sue-Ellen wore. By contrast, I did not aspire to live in a two-up-two-down terraced house and spend my waking hours going between a factory and a pub.

When I shared my thoughts and daydreams not everyone shared my aspirations. Some people really loved the idea of the small community spirit and the wholesome, hardworking imagery that Coronation Street represented. Some people thought I was fickle and wrong to want the luxury lifestyle. They saw me as having 'notions above my station'. Of course, I was also reminded that 'money is the root of all evil!' There is nothing wrong with either aspiration, but beware of people who criticise your aspirations – it often comes from their own limiting beliefs about what is possible for 'people like us'. People who are genuinely happy with their own choices will encourage you in your own – whatever they are.

Whatever we aspire to have, it is important that we make the desire our own and protect it from the values and beliefs of others. I have concluded that in life I would rather aspire to have and work towards my own list of desires and enjoy that journey than to settle for less and wonder about what could have been.

As we will also learn, the Universe works in mysterious ways and therefore needs us to do our bit in creating a vision or desire and holding it in our minds with the belief that it is available and attainable to us.

As human beings, we do not exist on this planet only to survive each day and lurch from meal to meal. We have an opportunity to use our intelligence and self-awareness to direct our energy to create, co-create, educate, develop, manifest and enjoy our time. We are able to quickly assimilate how best to use developed resources and technologies to create and invent things that only years ago were not possible or even imaginable.

Many people choose to live simple, uncomplicated lives where they have gone 'back to nature' because they seek to minimise their carbon footprint and enjoy a natural way of life. Others will face a daily struggle, not knowing where their next meal or money will come from. Some will live in a space somewhere between the two, and others again will live lives of luxury and others pure decadence.

What separates people is their thinking. Whether it is conscious or unconscious, it is our beliefs and actions that result in our physical experience.
Therefore, it is essential to be aware of what we are focusing on, which leads us to the next chapter: **Secrets of Success 3: WHAT YOU PUT YOUR FOCUS ON IS WHAT YOU GET.**

Before we go to this chapter lets hear from Vhairi and see how she got on with the text and exercises in Chapter 2.

Test Drive 2

Looking at who I am and what relationships I have with people has been very intriguing. I have never thought about my relationships in this way. I can be guilty of taking certain things for granted, so this has been a great way to appreciate the relationships I do have. I really felt like telling certain people how much I value them after doing this exercise.

It has made me evaluate my own behaviour with the people I care about. I love my family, but at times, I have to go off and do my own thing. I think they accept this now because they can see the difference between me being happy and unhappy. I try to make sure the time I spend with them is quality time, and I think my relationships have greatly improved as a result. It is also liberating to know that I have a huge impact on whether my relationships are healthy or not. I have taken this opportunity to consider who is getting the most of me and whether they are the people I value the most.

Test drive exercise 3

1. Have a look at this list of roles and responsibilities that apply to many people in life. Now tick √ each box that applies to you.			
Son		Wife	
Daughter	√	Boyfriend	
Brother		Colleague	√
Sister	√	Grandson	
Friend	√	Granddaughter	
Cousin	√	Auntie	√
Employee	√	Uncle	
Boss		Girlfriend	
Nephew		Student	
Niece	√	Teacher	
Husband		In-law	
Other		Other	

2. If I were to ask you how successful are you as an individual, what rating would you give yourself out of 10? 0 is useless and 10 is fabulous
0   5   ✪ 9/10

I asked for feedback from some of the people I care about very much and got very positive, encouraging results from my closest relationships. I was surprised and pleased that my best friend, my sister and my parents all scored our relationships at 9 or a 10.

I took the opportunity to tell my mum how much I appreciate her and that she has been a good mum despite a lot of challenges from all of us.

This exercise also allowed me to look at some of the more challenging relationships I have and to figure out what I need to work on to make them better.

Like Jenny, I also attract people who want to talk about their problems. I have quite a few friends where that relationship works because they genuinely want to hear my advice. They will honestly think about it and they feel better after talking to me. At these times, I often share things about myself and talk about my weaknesses in a way I wouldn't usually. I want to let them know that I too, at times doubt myself and feel like giving up. I see these periods as necessary and if someone else is experiencing this, I try to help the person going through it feel that they are not alone and that like all feelings, this one will pass too.

I do love the way Jenny's friend, Deborah asserts her boundaries by making it clear that if she has given advice and the person hasn't taken it, she is not willing to give them any more of her valuable time and energy and I will definitely be trying this. The next time someone is trying to offload some of their negative energy on me in this way, I am going to gently let them know that I feel for them, but I cannot take it for them.

Now, if I can see there is nothing to gain from a relationship, I don't spend time on it. I bear the other person no grudge, I even wish them well and think compassionately about them, but being with certain people just causes suffering and I can't continue that behaviour.

A traveller came upon an old farmer hoeing in his field beside the road. Eager to rest his feet, the wanderer hailed the countryman, who seemed happy enough to straighten his back and talk for a moment.

'What sort of people live in the next town?' asked the stranger.

'What were the people like where you've come from?' replied the farmer, answering the question with another question.

'They were a bad lot. Troublemakers all, and lazy too. The most selfish people in the world, and not a one of them to be trusted. I'm happy to be leaving the scoundrels.'

'Is that so?' replied the old farmer. 'Well, I'm afraid that you'll find the same sort in the next town.

Disappointed, the traveller trudged on his way, and the farmer returned to his work.

Some time later another stranger, coming from the same direction, hailed the farmer, and they stopped to talk. 'What sort of people live in the next town?' he asked.

'What were the people like where you've come from?' replied the farmer once again.

'They were the best people in the world. Hard working, honest, and friendly. I'm sorry to be leaving them.'

'Fear not,' said the farmer. 'You'll find the same sort in the next town.'

North American folktale

Secrets of Success 3: WHAT YOU PUT YOUR FOCUS ON IS WHAT YOU GET

When I take my dog out for walks I often meet other dog-walkers. I live in Scotland and the weather has a tendency to be somewhat rainier and colder than where I grew up, in London. It never ceases to amaze me that the common language of strangers tends to be the weather and I can often quickly tune into somebody's frame of mind by how they view the weather.

I see a rainy day as a wonderful gift that feeds our plants and makes the grass green. It washes the streets and pavements and helps fill our reservoirs to provide us with water for all our needs. I believe that by maintaining this positive view of the weather it helps me to feel bright and cheerful. I often meet people who say: 'More rain today, isn't it awful! I was hoping to get in the garden and I have washing to put out. This rain is really making me feel fed up.'

So you have the same situation or event, yet two very different perspectives. My focus is on accepting the rain and seeing its benefits whereas my walking companion's focus is on what the rain is preventing him or her from doing and its negative aspects.

I know that **WHAT YOU PUT YOUR FOCUS ON IS WHAT YOU GET,** therefore I work very hard to focus on the positives. I have never looked back on a time of my life when I have been 'down in the dumps' and thought, 'I can't wait to experience that again,' so why prolong it? Your mind is good at reading your mood and then reinforcing it by helping you focus on everything to prove to yourself that you are right. We are very good at being right. We want to be right and put enormous amounts of energy into making ourselves right.

In the process of working with people and encouraging them to think 'big' about their futures I am often faced with a response of: 'Surely it is better to think small, then you have a better chance of getting small and you won't be disappointed when you don't get big.'

These people are good at talking themselves into many foregone conclusions and feel satisfied when they prove themselves right. They say to themselves: 'I'm never going to get that job, it's way beyond my abilities so I won't bother applying for it.' The outcome is no job and they have proved themselves right. And do they feel happy that they have proved themselves right? Of course they don't but they are satisfied that they were right.

Another example is: 'There's no point talking to him/her because he/she will never ask me out. I am not pretty enough.' The outcome is, no conversation and no date. Once again, they have proved themselves right, by proving to themselves that they don't deserve the things they really want. And it feels awful.

If having read this, you recognise that you are talking yourself out of many opportunities in life then now would be a good time to think about changing the way you think and talk to yourself. Imagine the possibilities if you thought to yourself instead: 'It would be a challenge but I am sure I can get that job. They'd be lucky to have me. It has to be worth putting an application in.' The outcome: the job application has been submitted and who knows what next, but at least there is a possibility of getting the job.

Instead of putting yourself down, you could say to yourself: 'He seems like a nice person, the type I would like to chat to and I am a good conversationalist, I will just go up and say hello.' Outcome: ice broken and who knows what else, but at the very least, you will feel good for having had the courage to approach the person.

In focusing on simple achievable steps we allow for action and movement. We also allow ourselves to feel good about ourselves because we have engaged in activities that are more likely to take us towards the life we want rather than staying 'right' and stuck.

Do you know that we could all change our moods simply by shifting our focus? Monitoring our thoughts and choosing to think positively is one way of improving our moods. There are other methods, and many people have come to rely on these other methods: Anti-depressants, addiction to shopping, alcohol or illegal drugs. Consider all of the side effects of these alternatives compared to something incredibly simple, free of charge and with no negative consequences: Shifting your focus. It is always available and it doesn't make your breath smell.

I regularly work with groups of long-term carers over a six-week period. When we first get together we do a feelings audit. This in essence means that the people in the group register how they are feeling week by week, on a scale of depressed to ecstatic. When they first arrive they are often feeling sad, very down or depressed. We use the **WHAT YOU PUT YOUR FOCUS ON IS WHAT YOU GET** principle in order to train them to be aware of how they are feeling and recognise what it is they are focusing on. Often, it is the less favourable aspects of their lives and the hopelessness of their situation that they are giving their attention to. They are encouraged to reset their focus and think about an aspect of their life that they are grateful for, or a person or pet for whom they feel total unconditional love. Over the following weeks, the attendees report a gradual improvement in their general well being and emotional state. Often by week six many attendees report feeling great, happy or even ecstatic.

Being able to recognise and acknowledge your feelings is a useful habit to develop. They are what they are: Good, bad, indifferent, depressed or ecstatic. Ask yourself: 'Is this how I want to be feeling?' 'Is this how I want to experience my life?'

If you are feeling great then that is good news. However, if you are sad or frustrated you can quickly change how you are feeling by putting your focus elsewhere. Simply thinking thoughts of gratitude, love or compassion will quickly help you to experience feelings of gratitude, love and compassion for yourself and others. And if you do this enough, in time, you will forget you were once feeling sad or frustrated.

If you don't believe me, let's try it.

Exercise 4: What you put your focus on is what you get

This exercise will help you to reflect on how you are feeling and where you are currently putting your focus.

1.   When it rains do you focus on the benefits the situation will bring or do you dwell on the negatives?
2.   If something isn't going your way do you think about the positive things the situation brings or do you dwell on what is missing from your life?

3.   Do you:
    a)   Allow external events or other people to make you feel bad; or
    b)   Do you believe only you can make you feel bad?

Write your thoughts and decide where you want to put your focus.

In addition to recognising moment by moment how we are feeling and in making a conscious effort to focus on the positive aspects of life we can also develop a daily positive focus and attitude of gratitude by repeating the following text morning and evening. It is made up of a series of affirmations. When you first read them, it may not seem like they are true for you. However, regular reading will help you to realise that they are, and you will increasingly notice that they are a true representation of your life because you are actively creating the life you desire by putting the focus on what you want.

Resetting your focus

Read the statement below every day for the next 30 days (or for the rest of your life if you enjoy doing it).

- I (insert your name) commit to my personal success for today and for the future.
- I experience abundance, health and happiness in all I do.
- I am happy because I choose happiness.

- I am healthy because I eat healthy foods and choose activities that help to keep me healthy and vital.
- I am abundant because I am a child of an abundant Universe.
- I focus on the things I want and I do all I can with the resources I have to make my dreams come true.
- I am grateful for what I have now, yet I am confident that my goals and dreams are in the process of manifestation.
- I love myself, I approve of myself.
- I forgive others for actions that have harmed me.
- I forgive myself for harming others and myself, even when I don't know that I have.
- I trust that I am loved and supported by the Universe
- I also trust that everything is exactly as it should be at this moment in time, even though there are times I find it difficult to comprehend why.
- I accept my role in my life is to be clear as to what I want, to do all I can now to help myself, and to be open, willing and active in the recognition and acceptance of my gifts as they are manifested.
- All is well in my world.
- Thank you, Universe (or God, Source, Allah, Brahman, or any other deity or description of the divine essence that you believe in).

Before you can **ASK** and **Place your order**, you must think very carefully about what it is you want so that you can state it loud and clear, with the confidence that you believe you can have your desired order. You must declare your order as a positive statement, focusing on what you want as opposed to what you want to avoid, for example: 'I want to be healthy, slim and toned' as opposed to 'I don't want to be fat and lethargic' or 'I want to enjoy collecting my exam pass certificate' as opposed to 'I don't want to fail my exams.'

There are exercises that will ensure you really clarify your **ASKs** on page 61 but for now why don't you start thinking about: 'What would I want if I had no limitations?'

Allow yourself to become aware of the things you are currently talking yourself out of. It may be material things such as cars, clothes, a bigger house, or holidays. It may be experiences such as happiness, love, fun, or excitement. Or it may be challenges such as a new job, a new skill, a hobby, or a new relationship.

What I am about to say now may seem contradictory, but I think it is important to say that when we are formulating our wishes, dreams, visions or desires, we must be mindful of the other people in our lives and indeed ourselves. It may be wonderful to have a chance to travel the world alone but if you are married with three young children, now may not be the best time to do it. You might be able to include them in your vision, or put your aspirations in an order of priority or importance. I know from my own experiences and those of hundreds of my clients that these wishes can and do come true.

So as a word of warning, **Secrets of Success 4** is: **BE CAREFUL WHAT YOU WISH FOR BECAUSE YOU MIGHT JUST GET IT**

When I first met Vhairi I experienced her as a bohemian hippy chick. During our first early discussions we appeared to have a lot in common, but different core values and aspirations. I have noticed changes in Vhairi so I am interested to hear how her understanding and application of Chapter 4 has influenced her thinking and being.

Test Drive 3

Doing this exercise has made me realise how far I have come in changing my perspective on things. Now, I look for positive things in everything. I focus on good news and on happy events.

People often talk about Facebook and say that it is all about people sharing their personal lives and problems or showing off and taking selfies when really their lives are a mess. I see now that Facebook is like life: **WHAT YOU PUT YOUR FOCUS ON IS WHAT YOU GET.**

You can choose which people and pages to follow. There are a lot of pages that are set up to share good news stories and incredible happenings around the world. I choose what I see in the news feed, so if I am seeing a lot of negative things, it is because that is what I am focusing on.

Test drive exercise 4: What you put your focus on is what you get

---

1. When it rains do you focus on the benefits the situation will bring, or do you dwell on the negatives?

When people complain about the rain in Scotland, you will hear me say: 'Yeah, but that is why Scotland is so beautiful.' There are things I love about the rain: sitting in my house reading or writing, the sound of it pattering on a skylight in an empty house, and walking in the summer rain.

---

2. If something isn't going your way do you think about the positive things the situation brings or do you dwell on what is missing from your life?

I have learned to look at the positives and when I am talking to other people I often talk about the positives in any situation. I do think about all possible outcomes of a situation and there are always positives. It can sometimes be difficult to convince myself that the positive outcome is the one that will happen. 90% of the time I see the positive in a situation, and I accept that even if I can't see one immediately, it will come.

---

3. Do you:
   a) **Allow external events or other people to make you feel bad; or**
   b) **Do you believe only you can make you feel bad?**
Write your thoughts and decide where you want to put your focus.

I used to be unaware of energy, and would easily fall into the vibrations of the people around me. I would even take on other people's feelings as though they were my own. It wasn't until I started looking at myself that I realised I did that.

For a long time I tried very hard to avoid all of the bad feelings I was picking up from other people by attempting not to feel anything. I tried to build a barrier between myself and other people. I tried to escape from my thoughts and feelings and purposely tried to blank it all out completely. I went as far down the path of self-destruction as I was willing to go. Of course, you can't blank it out, you only add your own suffering.

When I became aware that a lot of these feelings belonged to other people and that I could feel them, it was a remarkable awakening for me. I realised who mattered to me and what I had to do to have them in my life without their energy affecting mine. Of course, it started with forgiving everyone. Then by taking responsibility for all of the actions I had taken in my own life that led to me being unhappy and forgiving myself. I understood that irrespective of the energy around me, I am still the doer. In my life, I am the one responsible for my thoughts and actions.

I also realised that these people who I cared about were giving out such an amount of negative energy around me because they were suffering and in pain. I learned that I could help them by changing me, that that was the one thing I did have control over. So I decided to change the thoughts and feelings I had about them and about myself and stopped focusing on the past.

I love my family and my close friends very much. Full stop. No despites, no buts, no nothing else. I love them and I want the best for them. I understand that they love me and want the best for me. By focusing on myself and on letting go of the negative energy that we had been sharing with each other, I found a certain sense of peace. I could tell that simply by giving out a peaceful energy, by saying positive things and looking on the bright side, it cheered them up. I can't really do much more than that for the people in my life other than think of them with love and compassion. I learned the hard way that I can't fix them and I can't make them perfect.

I do believe only I can make me feel bad. It all depends whether I catch myself first. I can feel when someone doesn't seem to like me or if they think I am full of it. It takes a great deal of practice to tune out of things like that.

Work is often a place where relationships can be difficult. We are often forced to spend time with people we wouldn't choose to in normal circumstances. In many big organisations, there is a lot of work pressure and people are not always thinking compassionately about their colleagues. I have had insecurities about my intelligence and worth at work. I can take personally what I see as criticism. It is my ego that is hurt, not my true self. My true self knows I am worthy and intelligent. Eventually, with practice and compassionate meditation, I feel less defensive about feedback and happy in the knowledge that it can only help me.

I do understand that often these people who offer their feedback appear because I want to learn something, like how to put my point across in an assured way or how to answer in a measured and intelligent way rather than responding defensively or even seeming aggressive.

I have put the resetting your focus statement in a task on my personal Outlook. Every time I am on my personal computer at home, I read the statement. I have also written my own affirmations, which I say aloud every morning after writing in my gratitude journal.

Saying affirmations is a new thing for me. I only started doing after reading this book. I don't know if they work or not yet but it does help me to focus on what it is I am trying to achieve in my life or what it is I would like to feel about myself. And I now absolutely know that **WHAT YOU PUT YOUR FOCUS ON IS WHAT YOU GET**, so I understand how important it is to start every day thinking happily about the things I want to attract into my life.

'Destiny grants us out wishes, but in its own way, in order to give us something beyond our wishes.'

Johann von Goethe

Secrets of Success 4: BE CAREFUL WHAT YOU WISH FOR BECAUSE YOU MIGHT JUST GET IT

A few years ago, I went to a restaurant with my family. It had one of those indoor play centres and before we even arrived the children picked their food, so that on arrival they just ran off to play.

Rob and I sat and explored the menu and eventually chose the items that made us salivate. The expectation of the deliciously cooked home-style meals sent our food receptors on a gastronomic daydream.

A very pleasant waitress came and took our order, we paid for it and then we sat and waited and waited. This is not so remarkable. It is happening in restaurants around the world every second of every day.

I suspect, in the main, that once the waitress has taken the order we all trust two things:
1. The ingredients required to produce our order are in the kitchen.
2. The Chef knows how to combine these ingredients in order to produce the promised description - the meal.

When our food eventually arrived, it was not all we had hoped for. Some of it was as expected and the children had no complaints at all. My meal was acceptable. It pretty much looked like the menu description but it lacked flavour; so I ate the offering noting not to return, however my husband's food was not cooked to his liking and he sent it back for additional cooking.

This mundane description of a visit to a restaurant really helps to sum up the **3 simple steps in Drive-Thru Success.**

- Decide what you want recognising that we are filtering our desires through our senses and our hearts.
- Ask for it in the expectation that the Chef will arrange everything to your liking.
- Pay for your order and finally receive the food.

So throughout the **Drive-Thru Success** process we must be mindful and aware that when we talk to the Chef we do so through our heart and emotions. We may think that we are thinking our way through life, but research proves that it is our heart (which has its own intelligence) that is responsible for originating as much as 95% of our thoughts. We feel first and think second. This means that unless we learn to master the ability to control and direct our heart's desires then we are in danger of allowing our fears and hopes to randomly write requests that we are not fully aware of. We are sending instructions into the kitchen that the Chef is busily cooking, in order to deliver not only our greatest wishes but also our biggest fears. **BE CAREFUL WHAT YOU WISH FOR BECAUSE YOU MIGHT JUST GET IT.**

All of the **Secrets of Success** work beautifully in isolation of each other however the alchemy achieved by combining them is truly magical. As when baking a cake, when you combine **Secrets of Success,** they interact and miraculously behave in different ways, in the same way that yeast combined with flour and water creates growth and expansion. The **Secrets of Success** also have a layering or multiplication effect on each other as you use them. When you combine **Secrets of Success 3: WHAT YOU PUT YOUR FOCUS ON IS WHAT YOU GET** with **Secrets of Success 4: BE CAREFUL WHAT YOU WISH FOR BECAUSE YOU MIGHT JUST GET IT,** you begin to multiply the effectiveness of your ability to create your future.

The wish is the docket that gets given to the Chef; what you get is a result of the energy you attach to it. If you are completely focused on a dream, very excited by the possibility, believe you can have it, and keep your attention on the outcome, it is like putting your docket under a magnifying glass and making it so large that the Chef feels compelled to cook up your order first. But once again be warned, fear and worry have much the same effect.

I once worked for a boss who quite frankly wasn't very good. Every year at my annual review he would begrudgingly issue my report with as a low a rating as possible. Apart from being demotivating and hugely unfair, a poor rating could also affect me financially as the annual pay rise and bonus payment was calculated against the report rating. For weeks prior to my meeting I focused on how badly it was going to go and how poor I would be as a result of my bad marking. A couple of days before the dreaded performance review approached and I was due to see my boss, a colleague suggested to me that I was in danger of creating a self-fulfilling prophecy and that I should go in prepared to argue a much higher mark and make it difficult for my boss to mark me down.

I then spent the next two days collating evidence to support why I deserved the highest possible marking. Over the two days my confidence began to grow and I started to believe it really was possible to influence my score. When I finally went into the meeting, my boss as expected suggested I deserved a 4 marking (5 was the lowest possible). I reacted with surprise and shock and even suggested that he was having a bit of fun with me, as we both knew how well I had done over the past 12 months and how hard I had worked. I then proceeded to remind him of the many achievements I had successfully managed to deliver and finally accepted with grace a 2 marking (1 being the highest possible). This was when I decided that the **Secrets of Success number 5** was very true:

IF YOU WANT TO PREDICT YOUR FUTURE, CREATE IT -

and I also learned that if I didn't **ASK,** people would not know how to help me achieve my goals and desires.

I am curious to discover how Vhairi has got on with **Secrets of Success 3:**
BE CAREFUL WHAT YOU WISH FOR BECAUSE YOU MIGHT JUST GET IT.

Test Drive 4

I love this chapter, because no one can deny how true it is. We have all had experiences where you have asked for something and when you have received it, it comes in a very exaggerated form of what you were looking for.

Before I started planning and pre-scripting my day, in a previous job I found myself in the situation at work where I was either extremely busy to the point that I could not keep up, or had so little to do that I was terribly bored. Every time I was bored and had little to do, I would think to myself: 'This is so boring, I can hardly stay awake at work because I have so little to do. I am not being stimulated, it's not challenging enough, something really needs to change here.' Then a week or so later, before I knew what had even happened, one of my colleagues would go off on holiday, I would be asked to take on another project, another person would go off on sick, and I would find myself snowed under with more work than I could cope with. Then I would say, 'This is too much, I am under pressure, I can't possibly do all of this work, it really needs to slow down.' And it would – but right back to the opposite extreme again. I was asking for something, and every time, my **ASK** was being answered.

Now that I realise this, I try to pre-script every day before going to work. I write out or say in my head what kind of day I would like. Here is an example from my journal:

'Today I will have a fun, productive, flowing day. I will happily finish off most of my projects and happily hand over the rest to my colleague. I will begin to feel a real sense of completing things. I will be buzzing on a really high vibration. I will have an interesting meeting and I will enjoy seeing some of my old workmates from my previous role. At the end of the day I will really feel a warm, fuzzy feeling of accomplishment.'

That was from yesterday's journal, and I have to say my day pretty much went like that.

It has taken me a while to get used to pre-scripting and it takes a lot of practise to be aware of what I am putting out there into the Universe about what I do and don't want subconsciously. Sometimes I just want a surprise and I don't write anything, although that is rare for me. If something is coming up and I want to do well at it it makes such a huge difference to my confidence if I have written down how I would like to feel about it. So often, I will write before my yoga class things like, 'I will give a lovely relaxing yoga class. I will be confident and flowing, and everyone will enjoy the class.'

I sometimes struggle with the time it takes for my wishes to happen. Then at other times, I think that maybe the Universe decides that if I really want something so big, then I will need to be prepared. Like people who win the lottery versus people who put in a great deal of time and effort to earn riches. For example, maybe by the time a writer has received 13 rejections they have become much more skilled at their craft and resilient to criticism.

'Everything is energy and that is all there is to it. Match the frequency of the reality you want and you cannot help but get that reality. It can be no other way. This is not philosophy. This is physics.'

Albert Einstein

Secrets of Success 5: IF YOU WANT TO PREDICT YOUR FUTURE, CREATE IT

Most people I meet are lovely, good people. They have lived good lives doing what they believe is right for themselves and their families. Many have studied hard and gained qualifications in order to achieve success in their jobs. Many have bought houses and struggled to pay mortgages for 25 years whilst making pension contributions for 40 years in order to enjoy their retirement. They retire at 60 and then have the decency to pass away by 70 in order to keep the strain on the NHS and the elderly care system to a minimum and maybe leave some inheritance behind for their children. I don't say this in judgement. I admire each and every one of them. However, they do this because modern society tells them that this is the best way to do it.

Many of these people - and I have met and worked with a lot of them, are working hard in the now, in the hope that someone will notice and offer them a bonus for working hard or a promotion so that they can use their wonderful skills and gained knowledge. What they don't understand is that, if they were clear for themselves what it was that they wanted for their future, then they would be contributing to the acceleration of achieving their promotion or bonus. They would be both energetically and physically communicating their intention or desire and therefore they would be actively creating it rather then passively hoping it would happen.

Any successful sportsman or business owner will tell you that unless you are crystal clear on your goal for the future then you will be unable to create a plan to achieve it. Well, life is the same.

We will explore in more detail in **Secrets of Success 7: END WITH THE START IN MIND, START WITH THE END IN HEART!** how our energy vibration, particularly if we are excited or jazzed up, can magnify and accelerate our manifesting ability and speed. So the following exercises are to be created by both visualising and feeling at the same time.

In order for our Chef to be able to collect all the ingredients needed to cook up your order for life, you need to be able to say very loudly and clearly exactly what it is that you want. When deciding what you want you must do so free from any limitations. As with gravity you are subject to this rule with no exceptions.

Nobody is judging you except yourself. So go for it. What do you really, really, want? One small word of warning, always remember **Secrets of Success 4: BE CAREFUL WHAT YOU WISH FOR BECAUSE YOU MIGHT JUST GET IT.**

If you are in a long-term relationship it can be very useful to discuss this with your partner. Ideally, you should share a similar set of wants for the future. If you are in a loving relationship, I will presume that your vision for the future will include your partner, so it is important that they are aware of what role you see for them. The last thing you want is for your dreams of world travel to clash with their dream of opening a bed and breakfast on the coast in your local town.

When asked, 'What is it you really want?' Many people are unable to think of anything other than, 'To be happy.' In principle there is nothing wrong with this. However, these people are robbing themselves of the chance to have so much more and rarely do they feel happy, because they don't have a clear idea of what that means to them.

Interestingly, in my experience as a coach, people are actually very good at telling me what they don't want. They are acutely aware of what is making them unhappy and can reel off a long list of 'don't wants!' This however, is what they are focusing their energy on. You don't want to do that, you want to focus your energy on what you do want.

The exercises on the next two pages are designed to help you get in touch with your do wants, but first complete your don't want page. Write as many as you can and don't forget emotions. For example, I don't want to be hurt, sad, abused, angry, undervalued, underpaid. Keep going until every negative thought or experience past or present is on the page. Use a separate sheet of paper if necessary. When you have finished it, and after you have used it to help enrich your do want page, you can tear it out of the book and throw it away or burn it.

Complete the do want page in the same way. Imagine you have a Fairy Godmother and she has asked you for a list of every single one of your hearts desires. Once again do not evaluate your list, just let your hopes and dreams flow.

Exercise 5a – Wants and Don't Wants

Things I 'don't want'
Things I 'do want'

So now you have some clarity as to what some of your true heart's desires are. It can be very helpful to fast-forward into the future to have a sneak preview of what your ideal life will look, feel and sound like. Let's take advantage of a time and space excursion and visit the future. While we are there, we could decide how we want to experience life in the years or months to come. Once we have experienced our future happiness (I have taken the liberty of assuming you will be creating a happy future for yourself) we can return to the present and write it down. Let's take some time now, to do just that. It is best to allow yourself at least 30 minutes to do this exercise.

Do not restrict yourself, and remember the **Secrets of Success 4: BE CAREFUL WHAT YOU WISH FOR BECAUSE YOU MIGHT JUST GET IT**

Before you get started:

- Find yourself a quiet space where you can relax and take a few deep breaths in and out.
- It might help to play some of your favourite music in the background to help get your creative juices flowing.
- Close your eyes if it helps and start to think about the future.
- Imagine waking up in 1 years' time, then 5.
- If you can do that, see if you can imagine yourself in 10 or 20 years' time.
- You may want to pick a significant birthday 30, 40, 50, 60 or 70 or you may choose a significant event: your promotion or retirement.
- Go as far as you can but make sure you can feel the event, not just see it.

59

- Now experience how your life will be, at this time.
- Explore the future in every detail.

Capture your thoughts and ideas in Exercise 5b below or on a separate sheet of paper.

Some people find this exercise a lot easier than others. If you are struggling to think about an unfettered ideal future then here are some questions you may find helpful to ask yourself about your new future:

- **Where are you living?**
- **Who are you living with?**
- **What noises or voices are there? Children? Grandchildren?**
- **Are you alone or do you have a partner?**
- **What kind of house is it?**
- **In which country or county are you? Listen to the language being spoken, you may be surprised!**
- **Are you on holiday or is this your home?**
- **What are you doing to attract money?**
- **What are your achievements?**
- **What are your hobbies?**
- **What vehicles are on the drive or in the garage?**
- **Where do you holiday?**
- **If you were to introduce yourself to a stranger how would you describe your life up to now (remember you can create your list of achievements in this exercise, so have some fun)?**
- **How do you look?**
- **What size are you and what kind of clothes are you wearing?**

You may like to do this with a friend. If you do, give the questions to your friend so that they can ask you the questions and write your answers down.

If you are doing the exercise alone, once you have lots of ideas about your life in the future, open your eyes and start writing in the previous table or a separate sheet of paper.

IF YOU WANT TO PREDICT YOUR FUTURE, CREATE IT

You now have the information you need to craft your own personal vision. This is your order, which you will ask for at window number 1.

There are some rules that are helpful to follow in order to make your vision as clear as it can be:

1. Ensure all of the language is present tense: I am, I have, I do.
2. Ensure you really mean it!
3. Ensure it is filled with lots of vibrant energy and descriptive language, such as: I have a beautiful... I enjoy exciting...

I have provided two real example visions for you to look at on page 61. Client A is very top line and Client B (which is mine) has much more detail. There are two schools of thought regarding the amount of detail we need in our visions.

The School of Detail

This school believes that detail allows the Chef to cook to order, exactly how you would like it. The time, place, quantity, dressing and price. This school says that the more specific you are the more likely you are to get exactly what you want and the less likely you will be to reject your order when it does turn up. I have many examples of clients for whom this has worked well. One particular client had a fixed budget for a new house. They needed 4 bedrooms and wanted a specific location. Logically their specification in terms of size and location meant they would need to wait till they had more money because their budget was unrealistically low. They used this format and were very detailed in their vision. Within the month they received details for a house, which matched their specification almost to the letter at their budget price. They continue to live there today.

The School of Essence

The other school believes that the more you focus on feelings and generalisms, the more scope you give the Chef for being creative and coming up with variations to the theme. It may be that there is more than one way that you would be happy, or feel rich other than getting a specific job or winning the lottery.

When you work in feelings and generalisms you open up a whole Universe of possibilities as to what may come up for you. This is also helpful if you are still struggling to see or say exactly what it is you want. Generalism allows for your higher intelligence or soul to take care of the detail. Sometimes we really don't need to know and in not knowing we free ourselves from, as Robert Holden says, 'sweating the small stuff'.

I start every day clarifying how I want to experience my day, both in terms of tasks and feelings. This allows me to enter the day with a mixture of structure and flexibility that opens me up to a variety of outcomes and possibilities.

Whether or not to date-stamp is a similar debate. If you say 'By December 2018' and it doesn't happen by then you may be disillusioned and give up. You may also be delaying the delivery. We do not always have all the answers and it is not our job to try to come up with them. If we leave the date open, Chef may put your order through straight away and we may take receipt in hours, days or weeks rather than in years.

I use both the school of detail and the school of essence dependant on the client and the situation. Both can and do work. You do what feels best for you but remember **WHAT YOU PUT YOUR FOCUS IS WHAT YOU GET.**

Exercise 5b – Create Your Future

Living My Vision

Living My Vision - Client A

- I am happy and fulfilled with an abundance of time for my children, my husband and me.
- I am a happy, calm, joyful and loving mum and wife, enjoying every precious moment I have with my family.
- I have an abundance of money to maintain and improve my quality of life.
- I am fit and vibrant with a healthy body from top to toe.

I wake up every morning looking forward to:

- playing with my children;
- spending time with my husband;
- spending quality time with myself; and
- doing stimulating work.

I am happy in the knowledge that my body and bank account are healthy.

Living My Vision - Client B

- I am so happy and grateful now that I am enjoying financial abundance and freedom.
- I am a loving wife to Rob and mother of three happy, healthy children.
- I easily attract income providing excellent service as a world-famous coach. I am regarded as an expert in matters relating to personal performance, improvement, general well being and happiness.
- I am a highly regarded author and a sought-after speaker.
- I own a global corporation which focuses on the improvement of peoples' lives.
- I am a philanthropist.
- I love my life and life loves me, therefore I exude boundless energy.
- My life is abundant in every way.
- I am truly blessed and all is well.
- I live in harmony with all around me.

Thank you Universe   19/10/19

Writing Your Vision

You will notice that both examples of visions are written in the present tense. This allows your subconscious mind to accept that these requests are possible and it will then get on with helping you manifest your dreams. Have you ever noticed that before you think about buying something like a car or a type of footwear, you are fairly oblivious to the specific make or colour?

I bought a new car a few years ago, a Citroen. It was not a huge buying decision. I actually bought it in a rush after our family car had been written off in an accident. You may think this was a disaster but only eight weeks earlier, I had decided I wanted a new car. Eight weeks later there we are in a ditch having been forced off the road by another driver, their fault, yet miraculously nobody was injured. The car was written off and the cheque was sent to us within days.

I called my friendly car dealer and he sourced my new silver Citroën Xsara. Until he called me and asked if I would be happy with one I didn't really have any conscious awareness of their existence. I took delivery of it and since that day onward all I see are Citroëns, on the road, on the television, being advertised and in the papers for sale. Our subconscious works in the same way. It tunes into things that will help us obtain our vision such as people, events and places.

You can now write your own vision. I have provided you with some guidance wording to help you. DO make sure your vision is expressed in present tense language, such as I have, I am, and we are. If you are not sure how to do this get a friend to help.

Exercise 6: Creating My Vision

I am so happy and grateful now that I am ...

... **Thank you Universe.**

I came across this wonderful set of guidelines for painting your own picture of tomorrow written by Chris Ensor:

'Paint a portrait of life to be proud of that could not be sold for all the money on earth. Hang that portrait in your mind and understand it is ever present. Reflect on every brush stroke that makes all the mountains and valleys and rivers and skies the most beautiful in the land. Share your portrait with others but beware their brushes. Select only those whose brush will add to the beauty and structure of your masterpiece.'

Once you have written your vision of your future, or painted your portrait, protect it with every bone in your body. I am sure you already know loads of people who can tell you a thousand reasons why you should stop day dreaming or wasting your time. If you want to share your dreams with anybody do it with somebody who has already got what you want. They know how to get it. And they will probably be happy to help you to achieve your own dream.

Now that you have written your vision, it is time to see it.

When you have clarity as to what you want, another powerful tool is a vision board. It is also the most fun part of creating your vision.

A vision board is a poster or pin board of the visual representations of your desires. It can be helpful to cut out images, photos or words consistent with your vision and pin or paste them onto a page or poster, creating a collage effect for your future. Of course you can always add more or take some off if you change your mind. You can also theme your boards and have one for work, and one for home for example.

I have many clients who finish writing their personal vision and really feel the energy associated with it. Once they really believe in the possibility of their dream I say to them: 'Hold onto your hat' as I have seen so many seemingly impossible visions magically manifest in days or weeks.

A client recently described her perfect house, which she had not believed was attainable. When I met her 4 weeks later she told me that she found this ideal house and promptly put an offer in.

She was fortunate insofar as her husband also shared her vision for this dream house and together they were able to join forces and both take the required action needed to follow up on the **ASK** for their dream home.

Her own house sold within a day of being listed and she is now living in her dream home. She really did have to hold onto her hat. She dreamed, believed and very quickly through action achieved.

Congratulations. You now have all you need to complete Step 1 of the **3 simple steps** in **Drive-Thru Success**. So let's go to the drive- through. In the meantime, lets also see how Vhairi has got on creating her personal vision.

Test Drive 5

For a long time, being happy was all I ever wished or asked for. While there is nothing wrong with that, as Jenny explains, if I am not clear what happiness means to me, the Universe will not be sure what to give me. That's when I think it sends you lots of lessons and challenges, to help you figure it out.

Before I went to Australia, I wrote a list of all the things I wanted – it was the first time apart from Christmas that I had ever done that. Without realising it, I had written down a set of life goals. It started out with very simple things, like a slow cooker, a laptop, and it quickly escalated to going white-water rafting, going on a motorbike, riding a horse, and to meeting the man of my dreams. This was a list and not a sentence, as my neighbour Holly thought when she said: 'Vaz, I don't think the man of your dreams is going to ride down the town on a horse'. I am still waiting for that one and I never did get the slow cooker, but nearly everything else on that list I did or I received – including Australia, which was written at the top with stars. Shortly after this list, I wrote my bucket list and I decided I would tick it off at every opportunity.

Working through this list has meant that I have made some decisions that I might not otherwise have made, like spending a tax refund on going on a holiday to New York at Christmas, walking the Great Glen Way on my own, or hiring a car with strangers to drive along the Great Ocean Road. Before I would have thought about doing some of these things, but no doubt have talked myself out of them. Now if it is on the list and an opportunity comes up to do it, I have to do it. It forces me to have difficult conversations with people; it forces me to do things outside of my comfort zone; it forces me to stop taking money so seriously; and it encourages me to do things on my own instead of doing it only if a friend comes with me.

When I got back from Australia, I stayed at my sister's while I was deciding what to do. I knew for both our sanities and for our relationship, I had to move out, so I put out into the Universe one of my first big intentional **ASKs**. I asked to move somewhere in the country that was surrounded by nature, that was an old-fashioned house with a great view. I contacted some people about it including the man I used to work for and he suggested I rent a room at his place – a house that I absolutely loved and was everything I had asked for. I had never considered that that opportunity would come up, but I took it and I spent two years there in a house that I truly loved. Like everything, it did come with some other things that I never asked for like stress and negative energy. In the end, it was not permanent and I had to move out. At the time it was a perfect example of the law of attraction working.

As I mentioned in my introduction, the opportunity to write this book with Jenny shows how **ASKing** can work very quickly.

I had been working for a couple of years as a PA in the NHS after coming back from Australia. I had decided that I wanted to learn more about writing and that I needed to get a job doing it professionally. A job came up as a communications assistant in the NHS, which would involve writing and creative work. It would also mean that I would be using my university degree. I used all of the techniques I had been learning to prepare for the interview. I met with two lovely people for advice and coaching and I practised my interview repeatedly. I put my passion for the NHS and for making a difference into the presentation, as well as the knowledge I had gained from speaking to the right people.

One of the people I asked for help was Jenny. She had been kind to me in the past and had encouraged me to develop myself. I met with her and she coached me on the presentation and the interview. I felt a connection with her and she felt the same with me.

I got the job. It was the first time in a long time I achieved something I really wanted for my career. It was absolutely because of all of the self-development work I had been doing.

I had been in the job for a few months when I met Jenny again to catch up. I thought we were meeting for a friendly coffee, but when we met Jenny naturally (as she does) went into coaching mode and asked me what it was I wanted to happen next. I had been in the job I had desperately wanted for several months but was finding it difficult to fit in with the people I worked with. I was feeling inadequate and stupid. The job was also a secondment, and it would end in a few months. I needed to refocus.

Jenny asked me to write down what I wanted to happen following the secondment finishing. I had never told Jenny anything other than I wanted to get that job a few months ago. I considered whether to be completely honest with Jenny or not, since some of the things I wanted were not directly related to my job in the NHS. However we were meeting socially, so I wrote the following:

- Get paid to be a writer.
- Inspire people.
- Feel like I am part of something that is making a difference.
- Do something creative.
- Get part-time work with the NHS to give me more time to write.
- A good project with an end goal.
- Do something different.
- A new experience.

Jenny gave me some advice, and some exercises to do that would allow me to focus on what I wanted (which can all be found in this book) and to help put the wheels in motion.

That afternoon I spoke to a colleague who made a comment that encouraged me to arrange to speak to my line manager. I spoke to her a few days later and let her know that I would be interested in part-time work in case she had not considered that as an option before. She said that she had actually been looking into whether there was any way that I could remain in the job. She did not know that working reduced hours would even be an option for me, and this meant that there was another option. The following week she got the go-ahead to allow me to apply for a reduced hours position. Later I applied for and got the permanent position.

To be able to work part-time I needed extra freelance work to make up the money I would be losing. I met one of my clients around the same time who requested that I doubled my hours for her. That week I also started working on this book with Jenny. Nearly all of the **ASKs** on my list were answered.

Test Drive Exercise 5a – Wants and Don't Wants

Things I 'don't want'
To feel insecure. To feel stupid. To feel uncertain about what I am doing. To spend huge amounts of time on things I don't enjoy. To feel like my dreams are unreachable. To feel stressed. To be too hard on myself. To feel defensive. To feel limited by lack of time or money. To worry about not having enough. To feel alone.

Things I 'do want'
To have a creative income that I love and I am paid well for. To travel regularly. To have a permanent base that I love. To have a life-partner. To feel competent, talented and inspired. To work on exciting projects. To have autonomy with the work I do to earn money. To have a sense of fulfilment and accomplishment in my work. To have loving relationships with my family and friends. To have an abundance of money flowing in and out for the good of everyone. To feel like life is an adventure. To teach yoga. To have a rich, varied, exciting career. To feel confidence in my work. To feel calm and free. To achieve my goals and dreams. To congratulate and celebrate myself for my achievements.

Test Drive Exercise 5b – Create Your Future

For this exercise, I just decided to answer the questions Jenny suggested.

- **Where are you living?**

I am living in a beautiful house in the country with a huge, gorgeous garden. I have renovated it, it has a lovely writing room with huge windows looking out onto the garden that is abundant with luscious green trees, bushes and flowers that are all dancing with the wind and my music.

- **Who are you living with?**

I am living with my partner. He is strong. I like to just sit with him in comfortable silence, thinking that I have never felt more content. It is not loud, we don't argue, we have adult discussions about things. He supports me in my work. He is not afraid to tell me when I am being stupid, but understands my personality and when I need to be on my own. I love the way he looks at me. I can't help but smile. I am at peace lying in his arms. He is happy in himself, he is confident, he trusts me, and he understands me.

- **What noises or voices are there? Children? Grandchildren?**

There are children around, my neighbours, my friends and family, and all of the lovely people I have met in my life who have helped me. My parents are visiting, my sister and her husband and their children visit. I have a cat. It is peaceful. The sun is shining I am sitting with my partner beside me, his arm around me, quiet and content. We often have my friends from other countries and their families here staying with me.

- **Are you alone or do you have a partner?**

I have a partner.

- **What kind of house is it?**

It is an old house, with high ceilings and real fireplaces. It has wooden floors and a big kitchen. I have a writing room, a library and an office. It has a wonderful vibe about it.

- **In which country or county are you? Listen to the language being spoken, you may be surprised!**

It is in Scotland.

- **Are you on holiday or is this your home?**

This is my home.

- **What are you doing to attract money?**

I am writing and working on lots of different projects with like-minded people.

- **What are your achievements?**

I have published books, I have had articles published, I have had my work recognised. People have written to me to tell me that I have inspired and helped them. I have been a part of something that is changing the world for the better – an energy movement to balance out the bad things that are happening in the world. I do charity work. I am an ambassador of human rights, in particular for young women.

- **What are your hobbies?**

Reading, writing, yoga, meditating, walking, photography, dancing and playing guitar.

- **What vehicles are on the drive or in the garage?**

We have an electric or hybrid car.

- **Where do you holiday?**

I travel around a lot for work but we also holiday in places like Italy, France, and Iceland. We go on at least two holidays a year together. We are picking off all of the places on our bucket lists.

- **If you were to introduce yourself to a stranger how would you describe your life up to now? (Remember you can create your list of achievements in this exercise, so have some fun)**

I am a humble, happy writer. I have worked very hard to be able to work from home. I am always working on a book or a project, sometimes my story, sometimes-other people's. I also do some editing now. I write articles for *the Guardian* and for *Total Film*. One of my books has been made into a film. One of the books I have collaborated on has inspired and helped people all over the world to live the lives they want to live. I campaign for education and equal rights for women all around the world.

- **How do you look?**

I have one of those gentle, soft faces with smiling eyes. My hair is wavy and thick. I have a healthy glow. My face is slightly more lined but otherwise the same as it is now. I am slim. I dress elegantly, but with my own style. I have a quiet assuredness. I am completely happy with my face and my body.

- **What size are you and what kind of clothes are you wearing?**

I am a size 8 with a 26-inch waist. I have created a diet that suits me and keeps me energised and healthy. It is easy to stick to it because I love healthy, delicious food.

- **How do you feel (consider the use of the words love and joy and gratitude)?**

I feel content. I am settled in myself. Life excites and delights me. I understand myself. I feel loved. I feel such an overwhelming love for everyone. I am so grateful for every happy moment I have with all of the people in my life that I love. I have wonderful memories of all of the people in my life.

Test Drive Exercise 6: My Vision

I am so happy and grateful that I am staying in a beautiful home that I love with a huge gorgeous garden, feeling like I belong here. I can easily afford to stay here and I have plenty of cash flow for all of the things I need and all of the things I truly want. I have a lovely writing room with huge windows looking out onto a garden that is abundant with luscious green trees, bushes and flowers that are all dancing with the wind and my music. It is an old house with high ceilings and real fireplaces. It has wooden floors and a big kitchen. It has a wonderful vibe about it. I hold parties and gatherings here. My home is a hub of people and ideas. It vibrates a great energy. I work from home and I am incredibly happy with the choices I have made that have led to me own such a gorgeous home.

I am writing and working on lots of different projects with like-minded people. I have published books, I have had articles published, I have had my work recognised. I write articles for the Guardian and for Total Film. People have written to me to tell me that I have inspired and helped them. I have been a part of something that is changing the world for the better – an energy movement to balance out the bad things that are happening in the world. One of the books I have collaborated on has inspired and helped people all over the world to live the lives they want to live. One of my books has been made into a film. I am always working on a book or a project, sometimes my story, sometimes-other people's.

I campaign and do charity work for education and equal rights for women and everyone else all around the world.

I have created a diet that suits me and keeps me energised and healthy. It is easy to stick to it because I love healthy, delicious food. I do yoga every day I can. I can easily do all of the postures and I enjoy doing it. I teach yoga, and give excellent, relaxing classes that makes everyone feel wonderful. I go on yoga retreats and holidays, and sometimes I go abroad and teach yoga.

I am sitting with my partner beside me, his arm around me, quiet and content. I like to just sit with him in comfortable silence, thinking that I have never felt more content. It is not loud, we don't argue, we enjoy talking to each other about things. We have fun questioning each other. He supports me in my work. He is not afraid to tell me when I am being stupid, understands my personality and when I need to be on my own. I love the way he looks at me. I can't help but smile. He is happy in himself, confident, healthy and he knows how to look after himself properly.

I have one of those gentle, soft faces with smiling eyes. My hair is wavy and thick. I have a healthy glow. My face is more or less the same as it is now. I am slim. I dress elegantly, but with my own style. I have a quiet assuredness. I am completely happy with my face and my body.

I feel content. I am settled in myself. Life excites and delights me. I understand myself. I feel loved. I feel such an overwhelming love for everyone. I am so grateful for every happy moment I have with all of the people in my life that I love. I feel solid and that I am really here, now.

Thank you Universe

My experience has been that **ASKS** require two things that are simple to write in a sentence, but which I have found to be a huge challenge in practice: you have to **ASK** for them without wanting them too much; and you have to believe that you deserve them.

The more I go along, the bigger my goals and visions get. This is like a double-edged sword but Jenny thinks it is important. She explained to me that you should have visions and you should have goals and you should know the difference between the two. Tiny little 'you' seems like a small problem when you appreciate the size of the earth, and the earth seems like a trifle when you look at it in terms of the Universe.

Because I want to be a published writer, getting a job as a communications assistant and being a yoga teacher was doable. Yet there was a time when neither seemed achievable to me.

It helps me to think that in the grand scheme of things, everything I will ever do is so small in terms of the Universe. It helps me because it means everything is much easier than you think.

'Ask and you shall receive' is the rule, but you must learn how to ask and how to receive'

Gary Zukav

Step 1: ASK – PLACE YOUR ORDER

Imagine sitting in your car at the window of a fast food drive-thru. It is a busy Saturday night and there are lots of cars behind you. You drive up to that first window, wind your car window down and a voice says: 'Can I take your order please?'

You open your mouth and say: 'I would like a burger. Oh no, sorry, I will have a big burger. No, in fact, maybe I am not good enough for that. I will have a fish burger. I would like chips but I don't think my luck is in, so although I would like them, I won't expect them. I will only have a small drink because I don't want anyone to think I am greedy or that I think I am special enough to deserve a large one.'

By now you will have the queue beeping their horns at you and the server will be totally confused. The Chef will be standing, irritated and unable to fulfil your order due to the confusion you have caused. Of course, no one goes to a drive-thru restaurant and asks for what they want in this way, so why do that in life?
The good news is that now you have written your vision, you will not be stumbling and causing a queue. You are going to pull up to the window and confidently and assertively present your vision as written in Chapter 5. Congratulations, now hold onto your hat!

So let's put our car into gear and move straight to window number 2 and consider what we need to do to after we have ASKED.

Test Drive: ASK

I have to admit, that for a long time, it simply did not occur to me to ASK for things. I didn't think I could. I thought that life happened to me and that I had no real control over how it happened to me.

I started with that funny list on my fridge. It all felt a bit wild and reckless. My trip to Australia was very experimental and spontaneous. It led to some incredible experiences like driving a quad leading a huge herd of cattle in the Australian outback surrounded by dogs, horses, motorbikes and Utes. How did I manage to get myself there in the middle of that adventure? Because I asked for an adventure.

It helps me in lots of different situations to ask myself, what is it I really want from this? What do I really want to happen? Most of the time, the things I want are fairly simple and achievable. The bigger things take more work, but I have the attitude that says, why not me? And because of that attitude the Universe often answers by lighting all of the dots so that I can see the path that leads me to what I want. It doesn't just happen magically, I understand now that it takes ACTION.

Step 2: ACTION – PAY FOR YOUR ORDER

Wouldn't it be wonderful if all you ever had to do to get anything you wanted was to place your order and simply sit and wait? According to the Genie in the lamp, that is all you ever had to do: 'State your three wishes and your wish is my command!' There are times when this happens - as soon as you write down your vision and commit to attracting it into your life, it can suddenly appear. The time difference between writing my vision of the ideal relationship and meeting my second husband was a little over 24 hours!

I was on holiday in Mexico with friends. I was learning all about reconnecting with my hopes and dreams. I had managed to bury them very deep and pour quick-drying cement over them following a disappointing first marriage and subsequent false starts. I was determined never to feel hurt again and was actually very happy living a full life with my son, and enjoying a successful career.

This was when I met Meri. She was a wonderful holistic masseuse, healer and coach. She was able, after four sessions, to chip away all of those layers of concrete to get to the real me so that I could reconnect to my desires for a healthy, loving relationship.

Meri told me to write my vision for my ideal relationship, as I have asked you to do, and to go to a private place and read it out loud. I went to the beach and although I felt pretty silly, I followed the instructions to the letter. As soon as I had been honest with myself about wanting to find a new relationship, I was keen to make it happen.

That evening, my friend Lesley and I went into town and headed for the Zoo Bar on the seafront. We were enjoying our evening and when I went to the bar I noticed a young man who was also staying in our hotel. I had noticed him around the hotel and on excursions prior to this evening and I had registered that he was actually very handsome. However I hadn't made any effort to communicate with him.

At the bar I initiated a conversation with him and quickly established that his name was Rob, and he was Scottish. We got chatting and after a few more drinks and dances we got a taxi back to the hotel. We sat on the beach not far from the spot where I had just read out loud to the Universe the characteristics of the person I wanted to have a relationship with. We talked the night away.

At some point Rob asked me what I was looking for from a relationship and I told him. I said I wanted the whole fairy-tale but that I was a single mum and my son would come first. By this time I had established that Rob was 10 years younger than me and I expected him to disappear into the sunrise. He didn't. His response to me, having asked him the same question, was much the same as mine although he had a one-year-old puppy who would always come first for him. So here I was, 12 hours after giving my **ASK** to the Universe, sitting with the human manifestation of my **ASK.**

A year later, pretty much to the day, Rob and I returned to that beach in Mexico and said our wedding vows. Gary, my son, gave me away and Lassie, Rob's dog, was waiting for us at home. We have since had two more beautiful children, Megan and Aaron.

I still often reflect on how different my life may have been had I not met Meri. Who would ever have thought that at 38 I could find my ideal man, marry him and have two more children, all by talking to the ocean!

I didn't know it at the time, but what I was doing, was engaging in **Step 2: ACT.** I was in essence paying for my order by taking action. I could have written the vision and put it in my bottom drawer and hoped that my ideal man would turn up and knock on my door, sweep me off my feet and - hey presto - happiness. Now I know that **ACTION IS THE CURRENCY OF SUCCESS.**

It is difficult to think of anything, and I mean anything that doesn't require some form of effort. Even staying alive requires you to breathe, eat and drink. Even if you were to remain in bed and be served hand and foot, you would still need to put some effort into the process by opening your mouth, chewing the food, and swallowing and that is without going into the effort your stomach and internal organs take to digest your food and convert it into energy. Everything requires some form of effort or action. In order to have anything we have a price to pay. The price is the actions we will take to make it happen.

WARNING: It is at this step that most people falter. People can be very good at the dreaming, wishing stage, at creating wonderful action plans full of carefully researched actions and commitments. Many people will even carry out many of the first steps, but it is interesting how many of these people then find it difficult to retain their commitment and direction. They have created a beautiful vision and set up targets all around it, but they just can't seem to aim and shoot.

How many people do you know, (and I have been one of them) who commit to losing weight and getting fit? They join the gym and buy all the up-to-date fitness clothes. They even go to the gym, get their induction, attend a couple of classes and then a few weeks down the line… nothing.

Or they join a diet club, they download the app, they get weighed, they set a target, they buy the special cookbook, the special scales, they tell everybody, 'This time I am going to do it.' They may do very well for the first couple of weeks, and then… nothing.

- No visits to the gym.
- No visits to the diet club.
- No more weighing food.
- No more diet diary.
- No more early morning walks.
- No more getting off the bus one stop early.

Nothing!

Most of the time, the habit is broken when there is a very good excuse, such as:

- I was on holiday and couldn't keep it up;
- I was doing a project at work and didn't have the time; or
- these things just don't work for me because I am different (the best one).

There is absolutely no getting away from the fact that **ACTION IS THE CURRENCY OF SUCCESS.** The choice is yours. Victors act, victims are acted upon, and we will expand on this in **Secrets of Success 17: CHOOSE TO BE A VICTOR NOT A VICTIM.**

My promise to you is that by reading this book and completing all the exercises you are guaranteed to be well on your way to experiencing success in your life. However, I do need you to help me to help you. You will only do this by taking **ACTION.**

I have, for a long time, wanted to study in order to obtain advanced qualifications, ultimately to obtain a PHD. I do hold onto the dream to one day have a PHD, but I am realistic that at this time of my life with my current time commitments to my children and my business, I am not prepared to put in the energy, time or money to follow this dream. For now it will remain part of my vision as opposed to a targeted goal. I have started doing bits of research through my business, which will one day form part of my doctorate. So I am still paying the price through action, just in small steps.

ACTION IS THE CURRENCY OF SUCCESS works at a number of levels.

Firstly, while you are taking action you are keeping yourself busy and that in itself can create a sense of fulfilment. Taking an active part in improving your life or making things happen allows you to feel like a victor rather than a victim. You are being active not passive.

Secondly it is said, 'When you take one step towards God (or the Universe), she takes a thousand towards you'. When you are engaged in co-creating your future, you are at the same time engaging the wonderful powers of nature and creating all of those wonderful co-ordinated incidents or synchronicities we talked about earlier.

Finally, you are re-affirming to your subconscious mind that this goal is important to you and it will in turn support your efforts by making your actions easier or more enjoyable. It will refine itself and install a new self-esteem and self-image message that will support your sense of who you are.

If you have held an image of yourself of being fat and lazy, your continuous action will redefine that image of yourself as someone slimmer and committed.

During the paying-the-price phase you will have two entities in your head vying for your attention. These two entities are your old self and your new self. The you that you are trying to change, and the you that you want to become, your ego and your true self. There are many ways to shut the old you up: interventions like therapy, hypnosis and NLP interventions. In my experience, they can and do work.

Equally, the more you act in accordance with the new you, the more you will build up your self-belief and self-confidence muscles, resulting in the new you. Whilst one is diminishing, the other is growing.

Remember: **WHAT YOU PUT YOUR FOCUS ON IS WHAT YOU GET!**

Who will win the battle for existence, the old you or the new you?

The simple answer is the 'you' who you give the most attention to, the 'you' who you feed the most, the 'you' you are willing to fight or sacrifice more for. Remember, the old you will not go away without a fight or expert assistance. Ask any ex-smoker who has taken 10 to 20 attempts to stop.

The new you will benefit from a hearty kick-start but you need to be focused and resilient, particularly when the novelty has started to wear off. The winner will quite simply be the identity that you focus on the most. If even after all your best efforts, you find the old you creeping back up, you must definitely get some professional help. Get recommendations for a good local practitioner such as a therapist, counsellor, coach, NLP practitioner, hypnotist, priest, guru, slimming club, or personal trainer. The important thing is to find somebody who can help you regarding your particular issue. Do your homework. Get references and testimonials, particularly if you are going to pay them, check that you click with each other. It is important that you feel you can trust your practitioner completely.

However, before you start googling a coach, do the following exercise and apply some CBT (Cognitive Behavioural Therapy) of your own and see how well you do using your own clarity, focus and motivation.

Exercise 7: The L'Oreal List – Because I'm worth it

Goal:	
Because I am not worth it	
Reasons why I will fail or give up	**Action required to eliminate**

Because I am worth it	
Reasons why I will succeed or keep going	**Actions I will do to perpetuate**

Once you have your plan of action and are doing all you can with the resources you have right now, you are literally paying for your order.

Once you have your plan of action and are doing all you can with the resources you have right now, you are literally paying for your order.

Now is the time to keep your eyes and senses wide open, as you are definitely moving into miracle city!

It is probable that you will be so enthused and excited by your sense of expectation and hope that you will be literally vibrating at a higher level. This is often what leads to quick manifestations or beginners luck so...'Hold onto that hat!'

Whilst you are on this high vibration it is also a great time to take as much action as possible. In the meantime please don't fall into the: 'I'll only be happy when...' trap by following **Secrets of Success Number 6: ENJOY NOW IT IS ALL YOU HAVE.** But before we do so, let's see how Vhairi get on with **ASKING** and **ACTUALISING.**

Test Drive: ACTION

I am a typical Capricorn, I put a lot of time and effort into getting up that mountain, but often I will go the long way round and even make the journey harder than it needs to be. Sometimes it is really difficult to know what work to do and I can find myself sitting all fired up ready to do something but not sure where to start. I can often put off writing by telling myself I need to do other things. Once I get started, I always get into the swing of it and can spend several hours with my little fingers firing away at the keyboard.

The writing is not the hardest part. It is going back, taking out everything that is unnecessary, sending it to people, and then going back and changing it again that is hard. Even harder again is convincing someone to read it and all of the work that goes into sending it to people who might help you get it published.

For me, it is not just putting in the work that is the tough thing it is putting in the right kind of work. I could write every day for hours and I would be putting in the work but it would be pointless if no one ever read it. Yet there is always this apprehension of actually finishing anything because that means people actually have to read it and give their opinion.

It is important to keep reminding myself why I am doing what I am doing, and what the end goal is. Even when I am at my day job, the one that earns me money, I remind myself regularly why it is I am doing this, that this is what I choose to do to stay somewhere nice, eat nice and go travelling. The work I am doing outside of work is about my creativity and trying to build a career that involves doing things I love. At the moment I am doing both and I am putting so much of my time into both because I want to live a life where my creativity earns me enough money for all of the things I want.

The self-development work that I do involves a lot of time and effort too. I could argue with myself that I could be doing other things with that time, but at the same time I understand that I can't succeed without believing in myself. In order to write well and believe what I write deserves to be read, I need to be aware of and in control of how I feel. I need to be able to feel what I am feeling without judging myself so that I can write about it and it can help others.

I understand that there is a price to pay for everything I want. I try to be aware of that, and make sure that I am making decisions knowing what that price is and in the knowledge that I am willing to pay it.

Test Drive Exercise 7: The L'Oreal List – Because I'm worth it

Goal: I am a published writer	
Because I'm not worth it	
Reasons why I will fail or give up	**Action required to eliminate**
I don't believe in my talents.	Practice and take on board every piece of feedback I get until I get good enough.
I don't believe I deserve it.	Work on my feelings of worthiness through personal development. Talk to people who believe in me.
I am too afraid of achieving my dreams.	Visualise achieving my dreams. Meet other people who have had their work published.
I am not confident enough to persevere.	Just do something every week. Set targets to finish my projects.
I think it is too out there.	Watch videos/films of people who have achieved amazing things.
I will be lazy.	Plan my weeks and my tasks.
I will procrastinate.	Evaluate every night whether I could have done something but never. Decide to do it differently the next time.
I will let other people talk me down.	Get used to talking enthusiastically and passionately about my projects.
My ego will get in the way.	Meditate and review my own behaviour to be aware of when it is my ego.

Because I'm worth it	
Reasons why I will succeed or keep going	Actions I will do to perpetuate
I have a strong message to get out into the world that will help people.	Keep reminding myself what my stories are about. Remember why I feel the urge to tell the stories I tell.
The world needs more female writers.	Engage with other female writers and publishers, network with them. Keep informed about the statistics.
I want to work for myself selling my own talents, creating things and making my own money.	I will focus on finishing my projects this month and on ensuring that they get out there and in the hands of publishers who want to publish my work.
This is my dream, I decided I wanted to focus on doing something and put my efforts into it to see what can be achieved so that other people can be inspired to achieve things too	I will remind myself daily what my dream is and I will put the work in to finish my projects and to start to find publishers.
To prove to everyone who ever doubted me and myself that I am a hard working, tenacious, talented person who will succeed because I want to and I believe I can.	I will be confident and brave in the things I do and say. I will be courageous in telling people what it is I am doing and what my dreams are.
I am not afraid to fail. I am not afraid to keep trying again.	Every time I get a set back, I will look at the learning, and I will move on.
I am strong and resilient.	I know what I need to do to succeed.

'The most important decision you can make is to be in a good mood.'

Voltaire

Secrets of Success 6: ENJOY NOW, IT IS ALL YOU HAVE

Eckhart Tolle has written a fabulous book called *The Power of Now*. He explains how being mindful at all times, and truly living in the moment can completely change your life. It is definitely worth reading and developing a mindfulness practice if you don't already have one.

Now is where we are and now is all we have. What is behind us is gone, and we can't relive the past. What is ahead of us is yet to be experienced and we can't live in the future. When you really think about it, we can only live in the present moment.

I don't know about you but I am a planner. I wake up in the morning and my first question to myself is, 'So, what's the plan?' I do this because I find it improves my productivity tenfold and I would be very reluctant to let go of this habit. I increasingly find that in modern times, the pace of life and business is very fast. With ever-improving electronic communications, we are always contactable and 'on call' for the office, for family, or for friends. If we don't have a plan to start with, we can easily be pulled in so many directions that we are unclear as to what we were setting out to achieve in the first place. Sometimes it is the plan itself that can cause the tension, or at least clinging to a rigid adherence to the plan, or putting an unreasonable level of importance on the tasks in the plan.

Whenever I go out for the day and I leave my husband to hold the fort, I am always amused and amazed by how little has been achieved and how happy everybody is, especially my husband. Now, when I say how little has been achieved, I am talking about *my* list of 'must-be-done-now' chores as opposed to my husband's 'it can wait' list of chores. My priorities are often about running the home like clockwork and scheduling to do things once chores have been completed. My husband's priorities are about food and fun; he will inject a chore as and when he feels it doesn't detract from food and fun. He is much better than I am at being in the now and enjoying the moment without looking at the clock and thinking about the plan.

Learning to be flexible about the plan and protecting 'now time' can be the difference between happiness and peace of mind, and frustration and stress. Developing a commitment to regular detoxing from electronics can also provide you with valuable time and space to be. As a minimum, learning to ignore emails and instant messaging, or even turning our smart phones off can allow us to protect our space and respect the now. Whatever we are doing now, even if we are doing nothing (and doing nothing is a healthy habit to develop), it deserves our focus, attention and joy.

Practice being in the now and also practice being flexible about the plan, whatever the plan is. If you believe you are working to a deadline is it real or is it just yours? Can it be moved? Can it be extended? Would doing something different NOW be better than achieving the deadline - for example playing with the kids, talking to a teenager, listening to a friend or making love to your partner.

It is a shame to think that we use our holidays abroad to achieve what could be achieved everyday. We go away in order to free ourselves up from rigid plans and constant interruptions in order to be calm, relaxed and spontaneous.

Take time to be all these things NOW. It is still important to take time to understand our past, think about the learning from our experiences, and use it to heal and forgive, both us and other people. This ensures that we do not continually repeat unhelpful behaviours or patterns.

We have a tendency to spend too much time dwelling in the past - going over events and feeling the same pain and suffering we felt when they happened. That is not going to help. When we recognise that there is a pattern in our lives - for example, we are always spending beyond our means and getting into trouble with debt - then we may still have learning to do regarding our relationship with money or our self worth. In this situation it is helpful to revisit the past to help us understand our behaviours and patterns. We do so to learn why we are repeating the behaviour. It allows us to understand the pattern and then let go of it. In doing so, we change our behaviour now and therefore change what happens in the future.

The same is true for the future. How often have you spent many hours rehearsing or playing a movie of the future where all is doom and gloom? You are the central character and not only do you visualise yourself being sacked or your partner leaving you, but you experience the emotions and physical feeling of sickness and anxiety. The events haven't yet occurred and yet you give your time and energy to them.

Remember **Secrets of Success Number 3: WHAT YOU PUT YOUR FOCUS ON IS WHAT YOU GET.** It is in these dress rehearsals that we are creating our future. Do you want to give yourself a huge pat on your back when you say I told you it would turn out that way?

We are merely creating our own self-fulfilling prophecy. Our subconscious minds are literal and accept instructions from us without judgement. If we say I am sure I will feel awful, then our subconscious mind accepts this as an instruction to feel awful. It might not even be the original thing that we dreaded that is the only thing making us feel awful, we manage to attract or screen in new events that we can feel awful about.

Where you are aware that there is an event or situation coming which is making you feel anxious there is a simple process you can follow. It is simple yet very effective. I first came across the foundation of this process in Stephen Covey's *7 Steps For Effective Living*. Stephen tells us to 'Start with the end in mind'. I did for many years and put my focus on the outcome. 'What do I want to achieve as an outcome?' I would ask myself. I developed a **SMART** process to express that I wanted to happen.

- **S: Specific**   What exactly do I want the outcome to be?
- **M: Measurable**   How much of it do I want?
- **A: Achievable**   Do I believe it is achievable?
   R: Reasons   Why do I want this outcome?
- **T: Timely**   When will I achieve my outcome?

At this time of my life, like many people, I was working very hard to be a 'good' person. My focus was external and my measure of success was on achieving external goals or outcomes. Later in life I recognised that much of this striving and attaining was not making me feel happy. I was not in touch with how my goals were making me feel. I would often end up exhausted but satisfied. In time I did receive rewards and recognition for my efforts, but I was driving myself to be an even higher achiever and although I was successful in doing so, at a deeper level, I was not happy. Eventually I reworked Stephen's rule and came up with my own version: **Secrets of Success Number 7: END WITH THE START IN MIND, START WITH THE END IN HEART**

Test Drive 6

After Jenny's suggestion in this chapter, I did read *The Power of Now* by Eckhart Tolle. There was a time when I was sceptical about a lot of these types of things (self-development literature) and I would have thought this book a lot of nonsense, particularly when the author describes having an epiphany that changed his life out of the blue. However, I would recommend that you continue to read it since it has some really profound messages that can change the way you see your life and the suffering you experience. Since applying the principles you will learn in this book, I have developed a way of thinking that is: 'I can learn something from everything,' so I read the book with an open mind and with the intention of getting something out of it.

This book has really given me some clearer understandings of certain things that have been causing me difficulties in life. For anyone who also experiences hormonal depression, or intense feelings of any sort the week before they menstruate, I found the part on the female pain body to be a bit of an epiphany for me. How a man could describe how and why I put myself through such anxiety during this week is incredible, but Eckhart Tolle has got it so right. I am only beginning to understand just how powerful my mind is, particularly when I am not aware of what it is doing. He explains with great clarity just how your mind can affect every aspect of your life and how you can create pain and illness for yourself within it.

That means that the opposite is also true. If I can manifest physical pain in myself and I can attract unfortunate events and circumstances, I can create a healthy mind-body by being conscious of it, and I can attract the kind of events and circumstances in my life that will allow me to achieve anything I want to.

At the same time as reading *The Power of Now* I also read *Think and Grow Rich* by Napoleon Hill. These books have some similarities, particularly around how the mind works, and how it manifests in what we call 'the real world'. However - and Tolle does examine this - I have a bit of a conflict within myself about this. Part of the personality I have had in the past is that I am an all or nothing person, so if I like an idea, I embrace it fully and I try to live it. However, you might find like me, that when you start to become interested in personal development, you will talk to people who will recommend a lot of books. They all have similar ideas, but there can be conflicts. One of the biggest challenges I am experiencing with my learning is finding a balance between separate aspects of myself that I think are all good, but are potentially conflicting.

I consider myself to be a spiritual person. I believe in a higher power although I don't know what to call it, and I accept that I will never know in a human sense what it really is. I don't go for religion with rigid rules that are taken literally. I believe that there is a divine energy-force in everything in the Universe and that it links us all together. I meditate, I do yoga, I practice compassion, and I want to feel at peace.

I am also ambitious and I want to achieve great things. I want to be wealthy and have the freedom to live the kind of life I want to live, I want to have a permanent beautiful home and the money to travel around the world. So I spend a lot of time creating visions, saying affirmations, writing down goals, setting targets, and reading about successful people.

I also like the complexity of being human. I like feeling excited and exhilarated. I like thrills, adventure and doing whatever people don't think you should. I am rebellious, I like to push boundaries and defy convention. I want to live an extraordinary life. So, how do I marry these together to find balance?

I don't know what the answer is. However, I am telling you about it because I think it is important that anyone who starts this kind of journey understands that it is normal to be confused about what to spend your time on. I guess all I can do is consider how what I am doing makes me feel and make a habit of doing the things that make me feel good.

I started reading *Think and Grow Rich*, and decided to start getting up at 5am every morning to say affirmations, write a to-do list, read and exercise. I decided to really go for the practices recommended by all of the millionaires in Hill's study.

Then I read the *Power of Now*, and realised that I was spending too much time in the future. I was putting too much pressure on myself to achieve things and meet targets and I asked myself, 'Is this how I want to spend my life?' So I spent a few days doing less and meditated a lot.

I can truly sit and appreciate the moment, but do I want to spend my life simply and peacefully accepting the ordinary? Tolle recognises that people will ask the question when reading this book: 'So why would you do anything at all other than sit and appreciate the moment?' What I have learned is that even the striving, dreaming and visualising should and can be done in the present moment, and you can feel the things you want to feel when you achieve your goals now. If you put a lot of stress and pressure into your work on your goals, then that is what you will get with them, and that is not what you are trying to achieve.

I try to remember that my vision for the future is ultimately about how I want to feel. Achieving wealth and success is nothing if I don't feel wonderful about it. The best way to achieve those feelings is to feel them now, to get used to feeling proud and content and like I have a world of opportunities.

As for my rebellious side, again, it comes back to how doing certain things makes me feel. There is often a temporary pleasure that comes from being decadent, or breaking the law. It depends whether these things hurt other people or myself. Rebelling by taking drugs and trying to act like a rock star might be fun for a while, but ultimately, it ends as everything does, with how you feel when all the temporary substances have worn off.

What I am realising is that there are other ways to rebel. I can rebel in my very nature by learning my true power as a human entity. I can still rebel against any societal systems that are harmful to people or the planet. I can still defy conventions and norms by choosing to know who I really am and choosing to make no excuses for it to anyone. I am getting better at that.

I told my friend that I was thinking about doing yoga teaching a few years ago, she said, 'Do you get yoga teachers who drink wine and smoke?' We had a good laugh at that, but later I thought, maybe in the West that is actually what we need. I am not advocating drinking or smoking, but it absolutely does not mean you are disqualified from spirituality or healthy practices. I once thought that spirituality and yoga was a once and for all, give everything up life-change, and it alienated me from understanding things that have helped me to live my life more peacefully and happily.

Who says doing things to further your spiritual growth (as I believe all mistakes are) is sinful? Tolle believes, as I do, that actually they are lessons from a higher intelligence that will help you to realise what a miraculous being you are. The best thing I ever learned was: stop giving myself such a hard time.

'Knowledge speaks but wisdom listens.'

Jimi Hendrix

Secrets of Success 7: END WITH THE START IN MIND, START WITH THE END IN HEART

When I am deciding on my outcomes, goals or visions, I ensure I focus on how I want to feel. More than anything else, I use my feelings to help me decide what it is I really want. Will pursuing a goal really make me happy? Will the end result be worth the effort or the sacrifices I will have to make? Am I chasing a goal for the wrong reasons? Am I doing it for my family in the knowledge it will make us happy or am I doing it for my ego? Often when we are ego-driven, we forget the happiness of others and our true selves. In essence I think about who I am being on a day-to-day basis: happy, fun, focused, joyful, collaborative and successful (on a good day!).

If I go to a business development opportunity I am careful to ensure that I don't have 'closing the sale' as my primary and only objective. I use a technique called **positive pre-scripting** in order to broaden my outcomes and allow for a richer set of possibilities. In a business context I would think about what I wanted to feel about the meeting afterwards, before going to meet a prospective client. You can see an example below.

Positive pre-scripting for a meeting

At the end of the meeting I will:

- feel valued;
- have presented my company, my proposition and myself professionally;
- have made a good impression;
- understand the needs of the client;
- be able to meet those needs if appropriate; and either
- have agreed to do business with the client (closed the sale) ;or
- have arranged a follow-up meeting or agreed that we will keep in touch so that we can review the client's needs again in the future.

I often use this list to help me prepare my agenda for the meeting. After the meeting I check back against my original **positive pre-script** and congratulate myself for achieving so many, if not all of my objectives.

On a personal level have you ever spent hours or days sweating over a conversation with a partner, parent or child that you know you need to have? Maybe you have young children and need to go away for a few days and you are worried about how they will react to your absence. Maybe you have decided to control spending and will not be spending as much on gifts as you have in the past. In either of these cases it is possible, if not probable, that you will run the conversation over in your head - I will say this, they will say that, and then I will have to say this.

I did this a few years ago when I decided I would like to become totally debt-free. I reviewed my expenditure and set a budget. The budget meant changes for everybody. I initially rehearsed in my head a long, drawn-out debate with my teenage son where I had to defend my decision and fall out with him over the cutbacks. Catching myself using this old, unhelpful behaviour, I stopped that script and practiced a new positive one: at the end of this conversation, I will feel loved, valued, understood and supported by my son.

Sure enough, when conversation time came around, we had a lovely chat. He was very unaffected and couldn't see any issue with my suggestion. In fact his view was he would rather we all spent less if it meant I could work less. My outcome was totally in line with my positive expectation.

There are many other times when I have to remain focused on **ENDING WITH THE START IN MIND, STARTING WITH THE END IN HEART.**

When I find myself becoming embroiled in a disagreement, I have to catch myself before I get more irritated and or even indignant. My feelings are a result of believing that I am right or that I am being wronged unfairly. In these situations I have to consciously stop myself in my tracks and remind myself that I am contributing to the escalation of the situation. I will often, if I can, excuse myself. Perhaps I will go to the toilet or make a cup of tea. During this valuable thinking time I will check in and ask myself a series of questions:

- What is happening?
- Why is it happening?
- What do I not understand about the other person's situation or perspective?

- At the end of this discussion how do I want to feel?
- Would I rather be right than happy?
- If I take the other person's perspective can I see why they are upset?
- What is the best possible outcome I can hope for from this situation?

The questions run in an order, which help me to regain control of myself and become mindful of my feelings.

Exercise 8: Would I rather be right than happy?

Think of a situation that is worrying you and answer the following questions.

What is happening?

Why is it happening?

What do I not understand about the other person's situation or perspective?

At the end of this discussion how do I want to feel? Would I rather be right than happy?

If I take the other person's perspective can I see why they are upset?

What is the best possible outcome I can hope for from this situation?

Armed with these insights and decisions: What is the best action I can take now to help me achieve my outcome?

How many times have you won an argument yet at the end are left feeling drained? Or worse still, your opponent (who, remember, will have been your partner, child, family member, work colleague, friend, customer or somebody else with whom you are supposed to be building a relationship) has walked out and you are left feeling deserted or lonely? These are indeed very hollow victories and they often represent missed opportunities to really learn about your relationships and how you can best enrich them.

What is happening is that our ego is running the conversation. The ego is the part of us that wants to assert itself and be right. If we can stop long enough to allow our heart to become involved in the conversation, we may find that we can feel compassionate for ourselves and for others, and therefore that we are open to listening and working together for the common good. When we do this we often experience a greater sense of calm, peace and happiness. Sometimes you need to ask yourself: **WOULD I RATHER BE RIGHT THAN HAPPY?** Which also happens to be the **Secrets of Success Number 8.** However, first, let's go over to Vhairi and see how she got on.

Test Drive 7

Positive pre-scripting is one of the easiest things I have tried and one of the quickest to work that I have experienced. I do it every morning after I have written in my gratitude diary.

We had an important visitor to one of our sites recently, a member of the Scottish Parliament, and I was to represent our press office. It was the first time I had to do something like that on my own. I was to greet the press arriving and make sure they got what they came for while adhering to our procedures. I was really quite nervous. That morning, after I wrote in my gratitude journal and said my affirmations, I wrote down my pre-script for the day:

'Today I will be calm, confident, professional, warm and welcoming. I will make a positive impression on everyone. The visit will go smoothly and I will be able to calmly and intelligently cope with everything that comes up.'

That is exactly how it happened. Had I not taken the time to do that, I may have had a whirl of thoughts going through my head about all of the things that could possibly go wrong, and how I could have ended up looking stupid and incompetent (subconscious fears that my ego often tells me). Instead, I chose to look directly at the day ahead, and think about what I wanted to happen and how I wanted to feel. It worked.

My friend Kirsteen and I also exchange a few words in the gym in the morning about what kind of day we will each have. I can't tell you how good it makes Kirsteen and I feel when we have our little exchange. Some of the other people around us listen in and have a little laugh. I am sure they must think that we are barking mad, but it means as soon as we step out of the gym in the morning we are already vibrating on a high frequency. Thinking about how we would like to feel has made us experience those feelings anyway, and we take them with us out into our day.

Test Drive Exercise 7: Would I rather be right than happy?

What is happening?
I feel criticised and stupid when I am given feedback from people.

Why is it happening?
My expectations for myself are too high. I am not taking feedback graciously. I am letting negative energy affect me. I am letting my hormones overcome my control over my own self.

What do I not understand about the other person's situation or perspective?
People probably feel the negative energy I am giving out and may feel uncomfortable telling me when I have done something wrong, but compelled to because it is their job. Other people may have an insecurity about being wrong themselves.

At the end of this discussion how do I want to feel? Would I rather be right than happy?
I want to feel like I have learned something, but that I am respected and supported.

If I take the other person's perspective can I see why they are upset?
Yes.

What is the best possible outcome I can hope for from this situation?
That we can be friends and that we can learn from each other. We can have a fun working relationship. I will get better at my job and at writing.

Armed with these insights and decisions: What is the best action I can take now to help me achieve my outcome?
To take time to think and breathe before I react to anything. To assess my own behaviour with other people. To choose not to react to another person's emotions.

'Pause and remember – the peace you seek begins with you! When you consciously and consistently choose peace in your words and actions, more peace will appear in your life. Stop blaming everything and everyone outside of you. Make peace within your priority.'

Jenni Young

Secrets of Success 8: WOULD I RATHER BE RIGHT THAN HAPPY?

In the previous chapter I described my snatched sanity break where I quickly compose myself and return to the discussion with a softer more understanding stance. I find it helpful to reopen the discussion with a very powerful statement or question, something like:

'I can see you are not totally 'happy' (insert the appropriate feeling here). What do you want me to do now so I can help? Do you want me to talk, listen, offer a viewpoint or offer a solution? What do you think would help you most?'

It is my experience that most people want you to **LISTEN** to them first and foremost. Only after they have had their say, and you have reassured them that you truly understand their position, are they ready to engage in a discussion regarding solutions or your point of view.

I have often talked myself into my own solution when I have been allowed to talk through why I am not happy. Feelings are the domain of the subconscious. As I said earlier, the subconscious is always listening. It is waiting for its instructions to do our bidding. Once we decide how we want to feel at the end of anything, the Universe can start getting on with making it happen for us.

Remember Secrets of Success 6: ENJOY NOW, IT IS ALL YOU HAVE. Why spend valuable minutes, hours, days, months, or even years in disagreements with people, family or organisations when you can choose to let go of bad feelings and **BE HAPPY NOW**?

I am from a very large Irish family, which is scattered around the world. Over the years there have been many family disagreements, some resulting in years of silence, hurt feelings and resentment. It never ceases to amaze me how a funeral can result in instant reconciliation. There we are standing around the coffin and suddenly one brother will embrace another and say: 'Let's just forget about the past, life is too short'. Now, as much as I love to see this happening, it does somewhat jar with me when I think of the years of having to listen to the moaning of the hurt party or parties. I often think, 'If only they had decided to choose not to let the silly disagreement go on in the first place!'

The attachment to being right creates a need to justify and defend a single perspective and denies any possibility that there may be an alternative version of truth. This then creates and maintains the separation that in turn creates and maintains the hurt, anger and negative emotion that somebody, other than us, needs to be responsible for.

So in simple terms by letting go of the need to be right you can restore personal happiness and in doing so save hours, days, weeks, months or years... maybe even a lifetime of resentment, unhappiness and possible sadness.

While it is still fresh in our minds, hopefully reading this chapter has brought to mind some recent situations where you have chosen to be right rather than happy. Make a list of the person, the situation, and how you and they were left feeling.

Exercise 9: Let it go. Reflecting on times when you were focused on being right

Person	
Situation	
Outcome: feelings/impact	
What will you do to restore a sense of happiness or balance?	
What is the learning?	
What will you do differently in the future to avoid the situation?	

In each situation, you now have the opportunity to rewrite history. You can choose to be happy rather than right. Why not choose to either let go of the beliefs you have associated with the situation or person or choose to forgive the person or yourself and in doing so notice how your feelings and the outcome changes for the better.

As explained earlier, living by our values provides us with the clarity of what is important to us. This leads itself to **Secrets of Success 9: YOU CAN'T PLEASE ALL OF THE PEOPLE ALL OF THE TIME,** where we will learn how to balance personal success and happiness against the expectations and demands of others. But before we go onto that, let's go to Vhairi and see whether she would rather be right than happy.

Test Drive 8

I have to say that I have a lot to learn in terms of this chapter. I find it easy with people whom I don't have very personal relationships with, or with my close family and friends. I still find it difficult with people who challenge me. I don't particularly like conflict, but I also feel compelled to speak up when I don't agree with something. So, I force myself to speak but I find it incredibly nerve-wracking, so it doesn't come out the way I want it to.

I get very emotional about certain things, like political or social issues, but I think I have some different ways at looking at things, and if I could express myself calmly and confidently, keeping in mind what I want the outcome of the conversation to be, I could get more comfortable talking about the things I believe in.

A lot of the time, these types of conversation come about organically, and there is not a lot of time to prepare how I want them to go. I think I have a lot to learn before I can speak calmly and wisely about politics or religion. The good thing is, when you are having difficulty with something like this you tend to find the Universe presents you with lots of opportunities, or even a person in your life, that will regularly force you to practice!

Sometimes that other person may want to be right. And that's fine, but I need to focus on what outcome I want. And I do like having conversations that help me to articulate what I think, and that question the way I think about things. I always want the outcome to be that both of us feel like we have gained knowledge and experience from the exchange while remaining amicable.

I have many friendships where this is possible, and I find myself attracting more and more people with whom I can have a discussion on an equal footing, where each of us take the time to listen to the other's viewpoint and think about it.

I would rather be happy than right, but I would rather not just simply say nothing all of the time. I need to make sure that I am not qualifying my own behaviour to appease other dominant personalities around me.

Test Drive Exercise 8 - Reflecting on times when you were focused on being right

Person	Colleague
Situation	Someone tells me I have done something wrong.
Outcome: feelings/impact	I feel like I am being criticised or attacked and I act defensively, possibly even sounding aggressive. I become quiet and insular. I feel embarrassed and incompetent because I have made a mistake. The other person feels uncomfortable because of my reaction. Perhaps they feel like I don't like them, or that I think I know better than them.
What will you do to restore a sense of happiness or balance?	I will try not to react when I am given feedback. I will make a conscious effort to encourage and embrace feedback. I will thank the person for correcting me.
What is the learning?	The learning is that feedback is essential to my learning. I do sometimes make mistakes. It does not make me incompetent or stupid. I need to feel competent, confident and intelligent myself.
What will you do differently in the future to avoid the situation?	I will not react in the same way. I will consciously smile and accept the feedback graciously. I will not take it personally.

'Don't chase people.
Be yourself, do your own thing and work hard.
The right people – the ones who really belong in your life will come to you and stay.'

Will Smith

Secrets of Success 9: YOU CAN'T PLEASE ALL OF THE PEOPLE ALL OF THE TIME

One of the most useful habits to develop is to **LEARN TO SAY NO!** For many people this has to be one of the hardest habits to form. Having worked with people with low self-esteem most of my life, I recognise that the fear behind saying no is often that people think that if they do, they will lose that relationship. Somehow they are only valued when they are doing something for somebody. Saying no, kindly, and only when you need or want to is a very liberating skill. But in order to be able to do so you need to recognise where your true priorities lie. Who or what is truly important to you and in what order?

Look back on the list of relationships you came up with in **Exercise 3: Success at being someone** and reconsider the original order. Think about being really short of time. Maybe you are going to Australia for a year at very short notice and you only have 10 days to get your house in order and say goodbye to everybody.

- How would you spend your time?
- Who would you spend it with?
- Where would work feature?
- If you could only take a handful of people who would you take?
- Where are you on the list?

After considering these questions populate the following chart in the order of priority. When I first did this activity I had included some of my friends on my A list. It was suggested to me by my friend Deborah, that this was why I allowed my friends to dominate too much of my limited and valuable time. I was at worst giving them equal billing to my children and husband. She always thought it was best that only the very closest family made their way onto the A list. Since I put my husband and three children in my A list, my life is much simpler! If it is a choice between spending time with them and the type of invitation that feels like a social obligation, they win every time, (unless of course I really want to go).

Exercise 10a: Priorities

I recognise that the roles I have and want to have are:

A list

B list

C list

When I first did this exercise it was a little scary. How would I cope if I didn't invest as much energy into everybody equally and fairly? How would they cope without me? I soon found that like Deborah, when I become more focused on my own self-worth and priorities, I could kindly explain to people who wanted to talk through their problems at inconvenient times that:

- now is not a good time due to other priorities; or
- we have already gone over this ground and as nothing has changed, my advice wouldn't, so could we change the subject.

My friends didn't value me any less; they just treated me differently. Of course there was an adjustment period for everybody, but now my true friends and I enjoy wonderful, rich, balanced relationships. As do my extended family and business acquaintances.

The more honest I am with myself *about* myself, the more honest I can be with others. When I explain that my children and husband come first, the people that truly care about me always fully understand.

Another great benefit of doing **Exercise 9a - priorities exercise – part 1,** is that I have been able to review my Christmas card list and cull it enormously. I now send cards to the people I truly value and in doing so, it is not a chore but a pleasure. I look forward to sending my annual update (cheesy I know) and in return, hearing from the people I don't get to see too often. The arrival of social media solutions like Facebook and Twitter means we can now maintain light-touch relationships with many dearly valued and over-extended friends and family, which is wonderful. This means I can now truly dedicate my valuable time to the people and activities that make my heart sing.

Living consciously from our own values enriches our lives and allows us to really get the most from our time. I have already mentioned that it is important to act from a willing heart and this is the focus of the second part of the values exercise.

Exercise 9b Private Victories

Let us once again come back to success at **Being** someone. We now have a clearer idea of our order of priorities in terms of the roles associated with who we are being. But who are we *really* being in each role?

I came across the expression 'public charmer, private villain' many years ago and I guess my Dad could at times fit that role. If I am honest, I am sure I too have been, and indeed can be, one in my own way. What we mean by this expression is that some people can keep their emotions under control and be very courteous and polite in public. They can be generous and giving, kind and humorous. Yet once they are safely behind a closed door, they are mean and berating, bad tempered and slovenly.

It always saddens me that the old saying: 'you always hurt the ones you love' is a saying at all. The cliché about clichés is that they wouldn't be clichés if there were no truth in them. So how can we break ourselves free from this unfortunate trait? Well, actually quite easily.

I want you to consider the following descriptions and tick the ones that you can honestly say you are now, not just in public but all of the time. Then look at the list again, and think about which of these ones you would like to be and put a star in the second box. Then make a plan for how you are going to change your behaviour to act more like someone with that value.

Once you have completed my list feel free to add some of your own.

Exercise 10b

In pursuit of being congruent both publicly and privately:

	I am ✔	I will work on ☆
Loving		
Fun		
Good-humoured		
Generous		
Kind		
Gentle		
Fair		
Honest		
Compassionate		
Inspiring		
Open-minded		
Open-hearted		
Assertive		
Flexible		
Approachable		
A good listener		
Non-judgemental		
Reliable		
Tolerant		
Other		

Now you have a list of the behaviours you are being and what you would like to work on being. You know who you want to spend your time with and in which priority, and you know how you intend to conduct yourself at all times.

The next stage to influence those original **Who am I being?** scores will be to conduct a more thorough audit of each of your roles. You may wish to do this alone or with the person or group in question. If you do this alone go to a quiet place and allow 20 uninterrupted minutes to complete the exercise.

If you have already asked for a rating during the earlier exercise in **Secrets of Success 2: I AM WHO I SEE MYSELF TO BE,** where it was suggested that 360° feedback could be of value, go back to that person or group and have a conversation along these lines:
'When I asked you earlier how you rated our relationship, you scored me a 7. What can I do or what can we do, so that if we were to review our relationship in 6 months time, you would score me a 9?'

Next comes the hardest part of all… LISTEN! Keep your mouth closed, your mind open and truly hear the words your partner, child, or friend is saying to you. It may be the first time you have ever asked and more importantly ever listened.

Now is a good time to introduce **Secrets of Success 10: THERE IS NO SUCH THING AS CRITICISM, ONLY FEEDBACK.** Before we do that, let's see how Vhairi got on.

Test Drive 9

I used to be a 'yes' person, so I agreed to every invitation I was asked to and spent a lot of time with people who were literally sucking all of the energy out of me by moaning, complaining and bitching. I ended up going on nights out and watching films that I didn't particularly like. I went along with everything in my life, because I had no direction, and no real sense of self. This contributed to how unhappy I felt at the time.

When I went travelling, it meant that for the first time in a long time, I was on my own, making all of my own decisions. I learned then that I could happily spend long periods of time on my own and that I could choose who to spend time with, and what to do. When I returned home, I no longer felt the need to say yes. It took some time for some of my relationships to adjust. I realised that it was tremendously important how I spend my time, and who with. Even my gym buddies have coined a phrase in my honour, 'channelling your inner-Vhairi' for whenever you want to say no to something. It's not that they think I am aggressive or anything (I hope!). I am able to say no in a confident, clear way that does not need an explanation other than that I don't want to.

Test Drive Exercise 9a: Priorities part 1

I recognize that the roles I have and want to have are:

A list
Mum Laura Dad Lisa and family

B list
Abbie Allana Jenny Bella Ryan Dot & Laurie Friends regarding writing or development Claire Gym friends – Rodger, running girls, Julie Work colleagues Linda Kate

C list
Other family All other friends and people I know Colleagues Acquaintances EVA

Test Drive Exercise 9b: Priorities part 2: Who am I being?

	I am ✔	I will work on
Loving	✔	
Fun		✔
Good-humoured	✔	
Generous		✔
Kind	✔	
Gentle		✔
Fair	✔	
Honest	✔	
Compassionate	✔	
Inspiring	✔	
Open-minded	✔	
Open-hearted	✔	
Assertive		✔
Flexible		✔
Approachable	✔	
A good listener	✔	
Non-judgemental	✔	
Reliable	✔	
Tolerant	✔	✔
Other		

I would really like to be all of these things, but I have to say that I am not at all times. I do think I show love to the people I care about, but I can sometimes get irritated with people. I do try not to express agitation, and apologise for it.

I think sometimes, my mother, my sister and I have a script that we have been following for a while and my sister can feel dejected when this plays out. The last time it happened I was immediately aware when her mood changed, and I felt terrible. I try very hard just to let her be who she is, to encourage her and to look for the positives about what she is doing. I am very proud of her and love her very much and I do tell her this a lot. My mum can be quite critical but we both react to it in different ways. I am more likely to answer with a smart answer and my sister is more likely to go in a huff. I do try to watch myself in these relationships, and have felt a great improvement in recent times.

I think sometimes I can be too serious. I am silly when the mood takes me and I like to have a laugh about things, but I think I can be too sensitive to the feeling that people are taking the mickey out of me.

I do try to be generous, and have become much more so, but I do think I need to work on that. I have become very independent and spend a lot of time doing my own thing, so I don't always think about things that other people might think of.

My family struggled for a while when my dad didn't have a job. I think it has taken us all a long time to feel that we don't have to watch all our pennies. My parents are still not comfortable spending money, but I have started to think about it much less. I do like to buy things and pay for things for my mum. I think about all of the sacrifices she made for us when we were young, and I think she deserves to be treated now.

This funny little thing happens to me with clothes. I lived next door to a lady who used to be a beauty queen, Dot. She is now in her seventies, but she loves fashion, and she loves clothes. She shops in vintage and charity stores, and sometimes I go with her. She has so much stuff, but she constantly gives things away. She has a friend with a daughter who also has a clothes obsession. She buys clothes constantly, and gives them to Dot, Dot takes some for herself and gives the rest to me. I go through them, take some things, and give others back to Dot. Every time I receive clothes from Dot, I have a clear out and give my own clothes to charity shops. We have a full cycle of clothes giving and taking! I have never had so many different outfits.

In the past I would have always insisted I pay half the bill if I was dining out with someone, but often the other person would insist on paying for the full bill. I know that they were doing this out of kindness, but I always felt like I was not assertive enough to pay myself, or I hadn't considered that I would offer to pay for all of the meal, so I would not be able to say, 'No, I will pay.' This often meant I left feeling like I owed the other person, or that they would think I was tight. Now, I decide beforehand if I am going to pay for the meal, and often I do. If it is someone I dine out with regularly, I might try and remember who paid the last time. But I have gotten into the habit of paying for things, and I can tell you that I don't seem to have a penny less for doing it. I can also accept things graciously, knowing that I will also be giving to someone soon.

Being gentle is something that I do want to work on. I am aware that I can come across as forceful, and deep. People who know me have said that I am a little scary. This is something that I was absolutely not aware of. I guess I can be intense, so I want to focus on letting people know that although I am passionate and opinionated, I am also very warm-hearted and inclusive. I am trying to be more flexible with people when they don't stick to organised events or times and to stop holding onto things that are not important, but I get so disappointed if I have been looking forward to something and I am let down.

This has been a good exercise to help me see what I am perhaps putting out compared to what I am feeling. I think my perception of myself is very different to the perception other people have of me.

'Between stimulus and response there is a space. In that space is our power to choose our response. In that space lies our growth and our freedom.'

Viktor Frankl

Secrets of Success 10: THERE'S NO SUCH THING AS CRITICISM, ONLY FEEDBACK

Once you have listened to the people who matter to you, you can decide what you will use to improve your relationship and park the rest. Listening doesn't mean that what is being said is always true for you. But at the time of saying it, it is true for the other person, regardless of the reasons why that person feels that way. They may feel that way because one incident has overly influenced their opinion of you. They may feel that way because of their own issues. Regardless of the reason it doesn't matter. How they feel, is how they feel. You need to hear the feedback and acknowledge the other person's reality. What is **very** important during this process is that you don't attempt to justify or defend anything being said to you.

The most important thing to remember is not to allow the feedback to hurt, offend or enrage you. You have asked for it and you need to be open to listen to it. Once you have listened you can choose what to do with the feedback: change, act or ignore - whatever seems right. A very useful tip is to remember that: **THERE IS NO SUCH THING AS CRITICISM, ONLY FEEDBACK.**

When I share this principle in my workshops or coaching sessions I am guaranteed to get the biggest push back from people who do not agree with this statement. This always amuses me because I had a wonderful teaching experience that brought this principle to life for me many years ago.

Carolyn Miller is an image consultant who first introduced me to this particular **Secret of Success.** Two friends and I decided to spend a day exploring our self-image, and paid for a session with Carolyn for what we thought would be a series of colour analysis exercises. When we arrived, she looked at us all and firmly stated: 'There is no such thing as criticism, only feedback.'

Now I wasn't too sure about this but decided we had paid our money, so in for a penny, in for a pound! In preparation for this day I had worn my favourite chic suit. If I had been honest with myself, I would have admitted that it fitted me better about 1 stone previously. It also had a short-ish skirt: not mini but short (in my mind anyway). I had bought it when I was responsible for client entertaining, but I had subsequently been promoted and now held a more senior post. Still, I

125

thought it would past muster, so when she asked for one of us to volunteer to undergo her professional eye, I was comfortable going first. I thought her analysis of my outfit wouldn't be too bad. In fact I was expecting some compliments regarding the unusual colour and youthful cut.

The ensuing 15 minutes really did test my acceptance of **THERE IS NO SUCH THING AS CRITICISM, ONLY FEEDBACK** to the limit. She started her analysis by asking me: 'How did you travel here today?'

Her consulting rooms were in the city so I answered, 'I arrived via public transport: the tube.'

I really wasn't expecting her direct response: 'Did you seriously travel on public transport today, squeezed into that awful skirt with your backside hanging out?'

Now if that was the opening shot, you can imagine the rest. I think I did at first intend to stand up and leave, indignant that anybody could be so harsh and cruel. But while I was being subjected to this awful humiliation, I reflected that she wasn't telling me these things to be nasty. She had no agenda, no vested interest in hurting me - she was merely offering me her perspective as a professional and I had paid her to do so.

That evening when I got home, I studied my reflection carefully and had to accept that her perspective was indeed very accurate. Carolyn offered me a plethora of 'feedback' that day, most of which I chose to embrace. However, I reserved the right to reject some of it and to this day, I enjoy wearing gold jewellery but not skirts that are too short.

It is only by being willing to ask for, and genuinely listen to, the feedback from the people in our lives (from those we know and trust, as well as those foisted upon us) that will we ever know what impact we are having. If somebody is generous enough to offer me feedback, I work hard to graciously say: 'Thanks for that feedback, I will think about it,' rather than my old defensive response of: 'Yeah but ...'

So, once you have received your feedback, if this is something you want to work on, you can start to create your action plan for improving those particular relationships. The first step is to decide what you would prefer they were saying about you. How do you want to be known?

Think about being a fly on the wall in 5 years' time listening to your mother, father, friend, child, partner, boss or colleague (you decide which relationship you want to work on first) describing their relationship with you. What are they saying about you? Remember this is in 5 years' time, so you have time to do all that is required to be the person you want to be and to create special moments and memories. Is the way they are describing you consistent with your own list of personal behaviours? Do you like what you hear?

From this snapshot of the future, what will you commit to do in order to ensure that this will be the way you are described at that time? Use the template on the following pages to capture your ideas and commitments, but don't forget to carry over the actions to your diary or planner.

I have completed an example of the one I did for my Dad many years ago before he died. What a wonderful gift I gave myself. If I hadn't followed this process, the last years of our relationship would have been pretty eventless. They would have been bland and functional, filled with duty visits and defensive conversations. Instead they were loving, joyful years, where we both benefited from the quality time, and we created lovely memories of my Dad for my son as well as for me.

When you are completing your own snapshot, be playful and have fun coming up with ideas to enrich all of your relationships. I have provided the first template for your most important relationship. Additional copies are available at the back of the book or from the resources section on the **Drive-Thru Success** website.

Exercise 11 – Relationship Enhancer

Name of person I want to improve my relationship score with _____	
How I want _____ to think about me:	
The things I will do to ensure our relationship is enriched:	
Action	**When: Date or frequency**

Exercise 11 – Relationship Enhancer – Jenny example

Name of person I want to improve my relationship score with: Dad

How I want Dad to think about me:

- Jenny is a loving, caring daughter.
- She is a daughter who listens and is willing to help.
- I am proud of her and aware of her achievements.
- I feel involved in her life, but I am happy that I am not responsible for it.
- I can go to her if I have worries or problems.
- She can come to me when she needs help.
- I know Jenny has time for me.

The things I will do to ensure our relationship is enriched:

Action	Date or frequency
Make time to call him every day and be prepared to stay on the phone rather than just check he is still alive.	Daily
Insist he joins us for high days and holidays.	As and when
Offer to assist with his shopping to save him carrying it.	Monthly
Offer to take him to hospital or doctors appointments.	As and when

Test Drive 10

When I was younger, I always felt like there was one thing that was really wrong with my appearance at any one time, and it was always something I didn't realise until I got out of the house, and then I would feel mortified because this one thing was so ridiculous that everyone would be laughing at me secretly. It would be like only noticing a mark on my shoe, or that a top was too low, or you could see my bra or my underwear. I see now that it was a reflection of that fact that I constantly expected people to be examining me and criticising me. In fact, people actually pay very little attention to what you are wearing, and really your mother is probably the only person who examines you in that way.

I do now consider who is giving me feedback and why, and I ask myself, do I admire this person for the things we are discussing? For example, I have a couple of close friends, Dot and Abbie, who know what my style is like, and I trust their judgement. They both know how to rock their own style. If I ever go shopping with either of them, I always end up buying lots of things I love. Because they know what suits me, they know me, and they want nothing more than for me to look amazing, and that rubs off. Not all friends or family members are able to be like that, they have their own insecurities that can't help but surface. They are not only thinking of you, they are comparing you with other people, or with themselves. The trick to looking amazing, is feeling amazing, and you only feel amazing in clothes you really love yourself in.

I have a pair of brown leather boots that I hardly ever polish. My mum hates me wearing them because to her they look scruffy and clunky. I like them because to me they look vintage and quirky. Lots of people comment on them. I don't know why, but I feel extremely me in these boots. I like to wear them when I am writing. It is as though they are an expression of my belief that you can be a bit scruffy around the edges, and still be really cool. I laugh about these boots, and to anyone who tells me they like them, I say, 'My mum hates these boots.' The whole conversation about the boots is a little funny expression of the relationship I have with my mother and our very different natures. My mum thinks everything has to be just right, tidy, polished, clean, and normal. And I have long ago accepted that I am a little messy, but there's a way to rock that. I don't want to be pristine. I want to be like an expressionist painting: if you look up close, it looks very messy and haphazard, but from a distance, it is textured and full of movement, emotion and passion.

I have been trying to take on board what Jenny says: not to take feedback as personal criticism. This is not something that comes easy. It is definitely one of my biggest challenges. But I am learning.

Exercise 11 – Relationship Enhancer

Name of person I want to improve my relationship score with:
• Mum

How I want Mum to think about me:
• I am proud of Vhairi. • She is a loving, caring daughter. • I feel at peace when she is with me, and happier and lighter about things. • She takes me places I wouldn't otherwise go. • I can talk to her about things, and she makes me feel better when she listens. • I am happy to know that she will take care of me when I get older. • I accept and love her completely for exactly who she is.

The things I will do to ensure our relationship is enriched:	
Action	**When: Date or frequency**
I will be more open with her, tell her more things, and make sure she knows that I appreciate everything she has done for our family.	As and when.
I will take more time to see her and make sure it is quality time. I will stop looking at my phone or thinking of other things when I am with her.	I will see her or speak to her every week, more than once.
I will take her places, and spend time with her. I will organise a spa night away for her, my sister and myself.	For mum's birthday (Completed)
I will talk to her about things. I will get into the practice of hugging her and making her laugh more often.	Whenever I am with her.
I will remind myself that she loves and accepts me just as I am and act as though she does.	All the time.
I will concentrate on being a bright, happy person for myself, and then she will be happy that I have turned out just fine.	All the time.

'Some of us think holding on makes us strong; but sometimes it is letting go.'

Hermann Hesse

Secrets of Success 11: LET IT GO

I think it is marvellous that our cars, washing machines, dishwashers and most of the electrical appliances we now own have early warning systems built into them to let us know that they are in decline or failing. Many of these also have computers that can run diagnostic programmes to tell us the root of the problem so that we can quickly fix it and restore optimum working. We know that if we ignore a warning light on our car, sooner or later the car will totally seize up and could leave us stranded by the roadside. The cost of recovery and repair at this point would be dramatically more expensive than if we had heeded the warning light and got it fixed earlier on.

So why oh why, do we ignore the emotional warning signs our bodies send out telling us that we need to stop and do some diagnostics to identify the root of the problem?

Worse still, why oh why, when we know the root of the problem do we choose to hold onto hurt and rerun stories in our head, deepening the wound, until we finally breakdown.

Not surprisingly, as with our cars, the cost associated with repair and recovery is also exponentially higher compared to the original solution, which would have been totally free of charge … The solution is to simply to **LET IT GO.**

I think **Secrets of Success 11: LET IT GO** has a symbiotic twin, namely **EXPECTATION BREEDS DISAPPOINTMENT.**

This lesson was taught to me several times as a young child. As previously mentioned, we were poor, and my mother and father (as did many in those days) tried their best to give us all the things they knew we wanted. I can recall asking Santa for a new bike at Christmas, a beautiful dolly, and a dolls pram. Not all on the same Christmas of course, but my parents, like many before them and since, went out of their way to fulfil my dream.

My mum was a beautiful energetic woman with a lovely Irish lilt. She would tell us wonderful stories and used words to paint pictures. I can remember her asking me:

'What colour would you like your new bike? If indeed Santa can bring you one?' I answered, a red one. 'How excited and how proud will you be with a grand new red bike?'

Christmas mourning (yes I then referred to Christmas morning as such) arrived and sure enough I had a new red bike. Well, it was at least new to us. The bespoke colour was courtesy of my dad's hand painting, which, I am sorry to say, was rather badly done using a thick off-red paint colour.

As young as I was and as innocent as I was, I was totally devastated and so disappointed. My expectations had been elevated through the roof. In my dreams night and day I had been riding the beautiful pillar-box red Raleigh, the envy of all of my friends, and here now, I was going to be the laughing stock of the street. So I, for the first time of many, put on the brave face and smile expected of me and masked the devastating feelings of crushing disappointment that I was really experiencing.

Another time I can remember coming home from school and my mum asking me 'Do ye want a wee sister for yer baby doll?' Now my baby doll was a beautiful chubby soft-bodied baby dolly. She had a fat smiling face and plastic arms and legs, not dissimilar to a modern day Baby Annabel. Of course I wanted a baby sister for her. 'Well go to your bedroom and you will find your new dolly waiting for you on your pillow'. I will never forget that look of excitement and pride my mum had. Here she was, able to gift me something and it wasn't a birthday or Christmas. How decadent.

I ran along the corridor and burst into our bedroom. There lying on the pillow was the saddest, most emaciated dolly I had ever seen. Her hair, which I am sure, had once been a beautiful mop of golden nylon, had been shaved or pulled away and all that was left was a shaft of matted mess that merely magnified the doll's distress. This poor toy looked as if she had just done 10 rounds in Sid's workshop from *Toy Story*.

I lifted the doll's limp body into my arms and try as I might, I couldn't bring myself to love her. In that moment I hated her, and my mother, for putting me in such a terrible situation. Once again I had to muster the fake enthusiasm for my mum's sake. In truth my huge disappointment was proportionate to my huge

135

expectation.

Throughout my adult life, I spent a period of time continuing to allow my expectations of people and things to set me up for disappointments.

Nailing this habit once and for all is a challenge for me; I still catch myself allowing my sense of expectation to leak into my psyche. However, I am so much better at managing my expectations and have developed a healthy **ATTITUDE OF GRATITUDE** that has enriched my life in all directions.

When I catch myself setting myself up for an expectation disappointment, I now quickly recalibrate and **LET IT GO** as quickly as I can so that I do not rob myself of my own peace of mind.

Another area to consider around expectations is associated with people. I sometimes hear myself using a term that I know I have adopted from my mother, a plaintive cry of: 'I really didn't expect anything in return…' quickly followed by: ' but you would have thought that they would have done x, y or z at the very least!' So I guess I did expect something in return.

When I reflect on many of my relationships over the years, I can now clearly see where I have let people down and where I have felt let down by others. If each of my perceived 'let down by others' was a red-hot rod of resentment held in my right hand, and my feelings of guilt for the way I have let others down a red-hot rod of guilt in my left hand, then I would go through life with my hands full of negativity and I would be unable to grasp the opportunities that come my way. By holding on I am only hurting myself. Far better to reconsider the root of the expectation and just simply **LET IT GO.**

I did this by examining each relationship and identifying the story I believed about the situations and events. Remembering the adage, **WOULD I RATHER BE RIGHT THAN HAPPY** and making the decision to just **LET IT GO.**

Through this process I have reflected on the learning from the situation and occasionally I decide to let the whole relationship go as well, but that is very rare indeed. I now have two empty hands, which are open and ready to receive with love and gratitude all the goodness that is offered to me. I now also have healthy boundaries, which I maintain while still being comfortable to say no.

Review your relationship list and take time to consider whether you are holding onto any old hurts, grievances, or wrongdoings or indeed any feelings of guilt on your side. Write down what you are thinking or feeling.

Then consider what action you need to take in order to, once and for all, **LET IT GO**.

Remember that your story is precisely that: a story. It may not even resemble the reality of the original events. If you need to do tangible things to resolve your past like paying off an outstanding debt or returning a borrowed garment then that is straightforward.

If you know you have behaved badly then a heartfelt apology can be offered, but sometimes it is ok to offer your contrition through thought and let your actions speak louder than words.

Exercise 12: Let them go

Name	
Holding on: right hand of resentment	
Holding on: left hand of guilt	
Action required	

Name	
Holding on: right hand of resentment	
Holding on: left hand of guilt	
Action required	

So far we have been focusing on the core ingredients required to establish our core vibration. **Secrets of Success 12: YOU CAN MONITOR AND MAXIMISE YOUR VIBRATION** is essential to supercharge your core vibration and to help you to create a wonderful daily existence and support you to achieve your vision, goals and dreams along the way. Before we amplify things, let's see whether Vhairi managed to let anything go.

Test Drive 11

Like Jenny, and a lot of families throughout different times in history, my parents did not have a lot of money. My dad lost his job in the late 80s when Margaret Thatcher was in power, and it became very difficult for my parents to make ends meet. I don't remember ever not having anything, so we were not as unfortunate as a lot of other people. We never had to eat sugar or tomato sauce sandwiches.

I think, unfortunately, we always tend to compare what we have with what our friends have, and some of my sister's and my friends had a little more than us, and of course we wanted to have the same. Some of our friends could afford to go on holidays abroad, and were bought expensive clothes, and the best Cindys and Barbies, while we were bought the cheaper ones and were taken on holidays in the UK. When I look back now and with such a wider understanding of wealth and of the lack of it in certain parts of the world, I realise that we were in fact wealthy.

It is just that in the west, we have developed a very warped view of what we need. I was never starving; we always had plenty of food. I was always clothed, and my parents could buy me new clothes. We always had gas and electricity, so we were never cold. We did live in a small house, and I shared a room with my sister until we both moved out, but we didn't have to share a bath ever. We always had a TV and we even had one in our bedroom. I could go on the smaller school trips but not the ones abroad. My parents could not have afforded to send me to university, but by that time we had a Labour government, and I was eligible for a Student Loan and I was able to go.

Like Jenny, however, at times like Christmas I asked for things my parents couldn't afford. Being as emotionally sensitive as I was, I realised very quickly that it was upsetting for my parents when they couldn't afford the things we wanted. I just changed what I asked for and by the time I was a teenager, I generally asked for a book, a CD and a DVD. If I got each of those, I was perfectly happy.

In truth, the thing I began to love the best about the presents at Christmas was my stocking (which my sister and I still get to this day). I think I loved all of the individually wrapped little quirky presents. They were so random: Kirby grips, lip balm, pens, stamps, stickers, sweeties, face masques, nail varnish, Christmas earrings, an orange, or a pound coin wrapped in Christmas paper. We had the stocking at the end of our bed, and when it was full, that meant that Santa had been, and we could get up and open our Christmas presents. I started to focus on the little things like that at Christmas. I think we loved it so much because my mum loved choosing gifts for the stocking, and we could feel it.

One of the best lessons I have ever learned in life is that you can't rely on anyone other than yourself for your happiness. This is not meant in a 'woe is me' sense. It is just that I found out that people, even my close family and friends, are actually very clueless as to what really makes me happy, so often without knowing it, they let me down. I made the mistake of putting a lot of hopes and expectations into certain people in my life when I was younger. I almost idolised people I liked a lot, but of course no one is perfect, so even these people whom I had held up high in my estimations, would let me down.

I could have missed out on the most important journey of my life if I had decided not to go ahead to Australia because I was supposed to go with a friend and she backed out. Because I decided to go anyway, I learned that if I want to do something, I am best just doing it. If people want to come along with me, then fabulous, but I am going to do the thing anyway. Actually, as much as I love my friend, I see now that I was absolutely meant to go on my own. I did so many things on that trip that I think my friend would have talked us out of. I took risks and made spontaneous decisions while travelling, and it was frightening, but liberating. I realised that I can do anything in this life, and that I can do it on my own.

What I learned travelling is that the one thing this earth is not lacking is people. There are people everywhere that want to talk to you, to come with you for a day, have a beer with you, smile at you, dance with you, laugh with you. If you have an open friendly way about you, people will want to be around you. For a long time, I think I clung to friendships. I was needy, because my biggest fear was that everyone I loved would suddenly decide that I had done something that was unforgivable and they would not want to be around me anymore, and I would be on my own.

Going to Australia, I let everyone go. I left everyone behind, and it was the best thing I ever did. Because emotionally, I let them go. Not in a forceful way. I had forgiven them all for anything they had done wrong to me, intentional or otherwise. I also started forgiving myself for anything I thought I had done wrong to them. Jenny's analogy was so true for me, I was walking around with two red-hot pokers of resentment and guilt, and I was not free to take any opportunities that came up. I was tired of holding them – they are heavy and painful. So I just sat them down and **LET IT GO**. That was the start of so many other things.

Test Drive Exercise 12: Let them go

Name	My family
Holding on: right hand of resentment	I perhaps resent the fact that I felt as though they wanted me to be someone other than who I am.
Holding on: left hand of guilt	I feel guilty about the way I made them worry about me when I was younger.
Action required	To forgive myself for the things I did wrong. To say sorry to my family for making them worry.
Name	Various friends
Holding on: right hand of resentment	I feel like friends often cancel plans they make with me and let me down.
Holding on: left hand of guilt	I only really feel guilty if I make them feel bad about it. I can feel angry if I let it.
Action required	I have to accept that people will always change plans. If it is important to me, I will let them know when we make the arrangement.

'The secret to longevity is to be happy. Every day a man wakes up, he has the choice whether he will be happy or unhappy. I have chosen to be happy.'

A comment made by a 102 year old man on *You Bet Your Life* when Groucho Marx asked him what the secret to a long life is.

Secrets of Success 12: YOU CAN MONITOR, MANAGE AND MAXIMISE YOUR VIBRATION

There are a couple of principles or philosophies that I find extremely challenging. At times I find it easier to deny their existence than accept that they are universal truths. Just because I find them difficult doesn't make mean they are not true, therefore if you also find them challenging, that's ok.

The first of these is that we are all energy and we are all vibrating. The only time you stop vibrating, is when you are dead. Our vibrations are like magnets. We attract things to us depending on the frequency we are vibrating at. When we are on a high or positive vibration, we are likely to attract positive happenings or to experience our reality in a positive way. Transversally, the same applies to low or negative vibrations.

How do we know at what level we are vibrating and how can we monitor and control it so that it is continuously giving us the best vibrational connection and pull? In simple terms how can we know what we are attracting so that we can choose the vibration that we operate at?

Given that we attract at the same level that we vibrate... what we put out we get back.

In the same way that cars provide performance data in the form of warning lights on dashboards to alert us to take action to prevent damage, the good news is that we also have a vibrational measurement and warning system called feelings. You may not be aware of it, but how we are vibrating is already embedded in our daily language. How often have you said things like:

- I am feeling down.
- I am low.
- I am not on my A Game.
- I am depressed.

These are all indications that we are vibrating on a low frequency.

On the other hand, if you are saying things like:

- I am buzzing.
- I am as high as a kite.
- I am great.
- I am ecstatic.

You've guessed it: you are vibrating on a high frequency!

The energy vibration management routine allows you to become aware of your vibration minute by minute, to monitor your feelings and notice when you are not vibrating at your highest level.

I think of myself as a tuning fork. I make sure that I am aware that I attract people of a similar vibration and that I will feel like I am 'not in tune' when I am around people who are not on my vibration.

Now, in principle, that is a good thing as long as I can respectfully remove myself from or avoid the low vibrational people. However, this is not always easy, or even possible, particularly if you either work with them or are related to them.

Whenever you go on an airplane, during the safety instructions you are advised: 'Put your own oxygen mask on before trying to help others.' This is also true for managing your energy. Get your own vibration high before trying to motivate others.

Like many of the principles in this book, understanding the ideology is one thing, but putting it into practice in a way that allows you to experience the very best life you can have, is another.

In order to assist with this I have evolved a daily routine, which allows me to connect with my vibration, thoughts and feelings, to put me in the best possible place to **MONITOR, MANAGE AND MAXIMISE MY VIBRATION.**

It is during the process of living life on a moment by moment basis that the opportunity to be influenced by events will either accelerate and improve your vibration, or catch you off guard and drop you into a low energy phase of frustration, anger, sadness or depression.

It is therefore essential that you establish your own daily **VIBRATION MANAGEMENT ROUTINE** and practice it every single day and monitor your feelings in order to maximise them.

The process starts in the morning as soon as you wake up. At first as with any new habit, this may feel time-consuming and clunky. However, I have learned to incorporate the steps into some other normal routines, like brushing my teeth, and they don't really take any additional time at all.

Exercise 13: Vibration management: gratitude

This exercise will allow you to set up a positive vibration through gratitude focus.

Gratitude

On waking ensure your first thoughts are those of gratitude. Write down 5 things you are grateful for as you enter your day (feel free to have more than 5).

1.	
2.	
3.	
4.	
5.	

Being

Now consider how you want to **be** for the next 24 hours. What would you like people to be saying about you and how you make them **feel**? (Some suggestions are: joyful, playful, happy, calm, gentle, focused, productive, loving etc.).

1.	
2.	
3.	
4.	
5.	

Doing

Now consider your priorities and your to-do list for today. What will you achieve and how?

1.	
2.	
3.	
4.	
5.	

Exercise 13: Vibration Management: Meditation

Meditation

Now would be a good time to meditate. Even if you can only manage 5 minutes, it will help deliver your intentions to the Universe. If you currently have a meditation practice or mantra, continue with that. If you are new to meditation, you could try by focusing on forgiveness or compassionate meditation. For a list of recommended books and Apps on meditation, see the back of this book.

However, for forgiveness meditation, you can start by saying gently to yourself on the in-breathe, 'I'm sorry,' on the out-breathe, 'I forgive you,' on the in breathe again, 'I love you' and as you breathe out, 'I let it go.' It is very common if you haven't done this before to feel very emotional when you do this for yourself for the few times – many of us are not used to showing and feeling that kind of love and forgiveness for ourselves. This will pass, and you will feel more peaceful afterwards. Then go on to think of anyone who you know is suffering, and do the same for them, then for someone who you feel has done you wrong, and even someone who has hurt you greatly. You may not be able to say it to them in real life – they may have passed on, or the pain might be too much for you, but putting that vibration will ease your pain.

A great compassionate meditation recommended by Torey Hayden at Samye Ling Buddhist Monastery in Dumfries is the loving-kindness meditation. Again start with yourself, and as you take deep breaths in and out (one for each statement) say: 'I am safe, I am healthy, I am happy and I am living with ease.'

When you are doing this for other people, you can say: 'You are safe, you are healthy, you are happy and you are living with ease.'

Try to imagine the person feeling these things. Do it with someone you like very much, someone who is suffering, someone who you don't particularly like or who is causing you difficulty, someone you don't know, and if you feel ready for it, someone who has caused you pain – but take small steps with this. You can then extend to do it for all the people and beings in the world – a beautiful meditation of peace and love for mankind.

Exercise 13: Vibration Management: More Gratitude

More gratitude! Notice and thank the Universe.

As you go through the day look out for evidence that you are manifesting your ideal day. Each time one of your desired **Doing** outcomes is experienced say: **'Thank you Universe!'**

Bedtime routine:

1. Review your day and congratulate yourself on your manifestations and how you have managed to maintain your vibration.
2. Make a note of the known activities you have planned for tomorrow. Your subconscious will get a head start on organising everything in your sleep.
3. Finally, write down 5 gratitudes and repeat these in your mind as a mantra that will take you into a deep and restful sleep. You can inject **more gratitude** between each one.

1.	Thank you Universe for
2.	Thank you Universe for
3.	Thank you Universe for
4.	Thank you Universe for
5.	Thank you Universe for

Keep repeating as you drift off to sleep.

Test Drive 12

The **Vibration management routine** is probably one of the first things that I started doing when I became aware that I am a vibrational being, and that I could change the frequency I was vibrating at. I probably wouldn't have put it that way at the time, but I heard other people doing it, and it is so simple and easy to test. I tried saying to myself (usually in the car), 'today I would like such and such to happen'. I especially concentrated on doing this when I was about to do something that made me feel nervous.

I am always nervous at job interviews, but the last time I had one a few years ago, instead of focusing on whether or not I would get the job, and instead of simply reading and re-reading things, I arrived at the place of the interview half an hour before, sat in my car and meditated for 10 minutes. Then I thought about what it was I wanted to happen at the interview. I said to myself: 'I want the people interviewing me to think that I am confident and passionate about the subject I am speaking about, I want to do my presentation first, and then feel at ease to talk to my interviewers as though they are my equals. I want to feel that the interview went well, and that I had a good conversation with the interviewers.'

I obviously really wanted the job, but I knew that in the past, I put too much pressure on myself when I wanted something, and I decided instead to focus on the experience I wanted to have at the interview as opposed to the outcome of it. The interview went exactly as I had planned, and I felt really good after it. I also got the job. Later, the people that interviewed me commented on how good my interview and my presentation was, and I put a lot of that down to the fact that I thought about what I wanted to happen before it.

I now right down in my journal what kind of day I want to have, and if I concentrate on how I want to feel, it nearly always happens exactly the way I script it. The whole day afterwards is so easy. It is in no way forced, because I am not putting it all on myself, I am asking the Universe to match the vibrations I am putting out in the morning before I go to work, and the Universe responds.

Gratitude journal

The gratitude journal is something that I have been doing for over a year now. Jenny has encouraged me to do it in the morning and at night. This was difficult for me to factor in at first, but now I manage to do this every morning before going to the gym. Along with the pre-scripting for the day, it sends out lots of lovely positive thoughts and vibes in the morning before I go anywhere.

It is amazing how easy it is to find things to be grateful for and it has completely changed the way I see my own life. It has made me think about how much I love and appreciate the people in my life. It makes me look back at the day and consciously find things that made me feel grateful. For example when someone gives me a compliment, I might just say thanks, feel happy at the time and then forget all about it. Yet it is definitely something I think about when I am writing my gratitude diary, and often when I think back, I realise that several people said something kind that day, and I get the feeling all over again when I thank them.

Test Drive Exercise 13: Vibration management: gratitude

	Gratitude
1.	Thanks for a deep sleep.
2.	Thanks for feeling fresh and at ease on a Monday morning.
3.	Thanks for the mystery of life.
4.	Thanks for teaching me lots of tools to make life more enjoyable.
5.	Thanks for understanding that you should just let things be.

	Being
1.	I want today to be busy and to be motivated.
2.	I want today to be gentle and easy.
3.	I want today to be funny.
4.	I want today to be peaceful.
5.	I want to be motivated for my writing projects when I get home.

	Doing
1.	I will get through my task list with ease.
2.	I will start writing the press release about the donation to the children's ward.
3.	I will be able to watch Game of Thrones.
4.	I will finish my tasks for Jenny.
5.	I will do an hour of freelance work.

Meditation

I say a mantra I came across in a book called *Joyful Wisdom* by Yongey Mingyur Rinpoche. I repeat this to myself to clear my mind of other things, and to help me remain focused on meditation.

Rest in natural great peace, this exhausted mind
Beaten helpless by karma and neurotic thought
Like the relentless fury of the pounding waves
In the infinite ocean of samsara

I also do compassionate meditation on myself and other people in the way that Jenny mentions in this chapter. I find this a very calming, rewarding experience.

"Good timber does not grow with ease: the stronger the wind, the stronger the trees.
The further sky, the greater length
The more the storm, the more the strength."

Douglas Malloch

Secrets of Success 13: WHEN I AM BEING CHALLENGED I MUST ASK MYSELF: WHAT DO I NEED TO LEARN?

This is the second of the principles that I find most difficult to understand and apply. It is said that when a person or situation is particularly challenging, a mirror is being held up to you. This growth opportunity, learning or healing is not meant for anybody else other than yourself. The question to be asked is: 'What is it within myself that is subconsciously being mirrored back to me so that I can learn about myself?'

A number of years ago I started to work with a very difficult person. I have since become an expert in that person's unhelpful behaviours and try as I may they continue to show up in my world holding up a mirror. For years I maintained it wasn't me it was them. Not once did I attempt to seek learning and growth for myself. I concluded that this person somehow felt 'less than' in my presence and that, although there was no need to, they insisted on comparing and competing with me.

One day, after an unpleasant incident, I took time to consider why I was attracting these experiences into my life. I explored the mirror principle and sure enough the answer presented itself. I had been going through a period of doubt and fear. I had been comparing myself to others and I had been endeavouring to prove that I was as good as them if not better. Now that sounds to me like comparing and competing. I took the opportunity to reflect on my strength and to affirm to myself that I was enough. Enough was all that was needed and enough was all that I could be. I also made a commitment to be gentler with myself and with others. I recognised that when I set myself excruciatingly high standards, I am unwittingly setting that standard for others and that can make them feel inadequate.

This kind of self-development growth work is not a one-time fix. It requires practice. I practice noticing others and myself. I practice noticing my feelings and thoughts. I practice letting them go and affirming that:
- I love myself.
- I approve of myself.
- All is well in my word.
- I am enough.

155

Another way to put this is, you cannot see in someone else what you don't have in yourself. If somebody has been brought up without being taught to say thank you and you gave them a bunch of flowers, which they accepted without saying thank you, you would probably think they were being rude or ungrateful. Now the fact that they didn't say thank you is a real opportunity to be curious as to what it is about them that has led to this behaviour. However, I suspect many of you will do what I have often done: berate their ungratefulness and wonder, in a whiney way: 'What did I do to deserve that?'

Well clearly I did nothing and paradoxically neither did they. However it is my attachment to expectation that leads to my negative feeling about the situation. We have covered this earlier in **Secrets of Success 3: WHAT YOU PUT YOUR FOCUS ON IS WHAT YOU GET** and **Secrets of Success 11: LETTING GO.**

Can you see that by judging this type of behaviour and going into a vortex of overthinking, you become what you are observing: rude and strangely ungrateful or even resentful of the original giving?

Each moment of negative reaction can lead you (if you choose) to accept that people are different, and take that moment to gently and curiously consider why you feel the need to expect something from this person. I have learnt to use the expression Namaste in these situations. Simply put, Namaste means the soul in me honours, respects and loves the soul in you. I may not understand you, however I don't need to judge you. In expressing Namaste I allow the release of the feeling or negative energy and restore myself to the state I want to maintain: on a joyful positive vibration. Namaste, reader x

Developing a practice of mindfulness in which you learn to notice your thoughts and feelings in each moment is a great way to keep your vibration positive. However, there are also times when it is necessary to put **Secrets of Success 14** into action: **AVOID PEOPLE WHO HAVE A PROBLEM FOR EVERY SOLUTION** Yet, before we go there, let's read about the challenges Vhairi is experiencing and what they are teaching her.

Test Drive 13

It really is quite funny how these things turn up. Only last night, I was experiencing this very thing. I was trying to explain to a friend (we'll call him Jim) about how the expectations he had of another person's behaviour was leading to disappointment for him. Jim was talking about a friend of his who he felt could be more generous and giving, but whose natural response to things is to be rather selfish. I was trying to explain to him that by trying to make a selfish person selfless, Jim was making himself agitated and that he would be much happier if he just accepted this person the way they were or chose not to have him in his life. In the end, Jim did not really understand what I was trying to say and we changed the topic of conversation.

I went to bed and woke up to this chapter for review, and laughed to myself. Not about Jim, but about myself. It made me realise that actually I, too, was getting annoyed about Jim's behaviour for not letting this other person just be who they are. I am actually trying to do exactly the same thing with him by trying to make him behave differently. I should listen to my own advice! Obviously I am seeing in Jim things I don't like about myself. Like Jenny, and like Jim, I have incredibly high expectations of myself, and that can mean that I have high expectations of other people.

I have completely accepted certain people in my life (my close friends and family) but with newer friends, I still try to shape them into the kind of person I think they should be with my well-meaning advice. Jim (who I might add is 40 years older than me) was quite rightly saying to me (albeit not quite so bluntly): 'So you think you have wisdom and experience enough to tell me how I should behave?' He is absolutely right – who am I to be telling anyone else how they should behave? I should listen to my own advice and let that person be.

One of the things I am learning from doing the exercises in this book is, all roads lead back to you! All of them!

'Avoid cynical and negative people like the plague. They are killers of potential.'

Rick Pitino

Secrets of Success 14: AVOID PEOPLE WHO HAVE A PROBLEM FOR EVERY SOLUTION

I have been practicing these principles for many years now. Although I have always considered myself to be a Pollyanna type of person, I find the daily routine and principles ensure I can maintain Pollyanna status most of the time. For those of you who are not old enough to recognise the reference, Pollyanna was a happy-go-lucky, sweet child who was sent to live with her childless maiden aunt. The aunt and many of the townspeople lived in a state of fear and judgement. They were insular and unfriendly, and consequently unhappy.

Pollyanna had a good heart and was full of love, fun and mischief - pretty much like myself. She befriended many townsfolk with her simple ways and expectation that her unconditional love would be met and reciprocated. Where it wasn't, she was curious, but brave enough to ask questions that sought to understand. She was the archetypal personal development coach.

In time she started to melt hearts and help people to make connections. However, her maiden Aunt remained cold and unloving. One day Pollyanna fell from a tree and was left paralysed. In the face of this setback and the subsequent isolation she fell into a deep depression. In time the Aunt decided to invite the townsfolk to see if their influence could help Pollyanna out of her depression and sure enough the love and positive energy of the town not only melted Pollyanna's heart but that of her Aunt also.

This is another example of how a positive vibration can influence the lives of other people and raise their vibrations, ultimately leading them to happiness. There are many Pollyannas in this world and I like to be with them. They generally have an air of optimism and will help you find a solution for every problem. In fact, they tend to have very few problems and lots of opportunities.
At the other end of the spectrum is the person who will find a problem for every solution. They are the 'Why not's' or the 'Eeyores' of this world.

I think the hardest thing about being in the company of the naysayers is that they seem to drain the positive life out of every situation. They are like happiness extractor fans. They are living their lives (as we all are) getting back everything they put their focus on. In their case what they are focusing on is: the how not; why not; I can't; never can; no one can; it's all right for them but we could never afford it; it's all new age thinking mumbo jumbo so I'm not doing it; I'm not that stupid, naïve, or weak.

When I have to be around people like this, and I try very hard not to be, I find it best to protect my precious ideas and dreams, so I either keep them under wraps, or provide the minimum of information. Otherwise they will provide me with a problem for every solution, a reason not to for every hope I have, and a negative for every positive. I also find it useful to apply a 2:1 ratio of positive to negative.

For every negative person who is in my orbit, I ensure I have at least two positive people. I have some über positives on speed dial and I will dial them for some positive reinforcement in the light of a negativity shower.
I find it really helpful to use my vision statement and daily routine, repeating my affirmations as a cloak of protection from the negativity that is trying to seep into my psyche.

I read recently that water cannot sink a ship unless it gets inside. This also applies to negativity. It cannot kill your dream or bring your vibration down unless you let it get inside your mind and start to believe the naysayers. I am not saying that you shouldn't seek counsel and test your ideas with experienced advisors. Yet, even this can have its flaws. Walt Disney was sacked because he lacked imagination. Oprah was sacked and told she was not suitable for television. Einstein was written off as a young boy, apparently lacking in intelligence.

Many of my clients find the neutrality of working with a coach to be helpful. A coach has no agenda and can be both supportive and challenging at the same time. Whoever you decide to confide in, make sure they have your best interests at heart and that you trust them. Also ensure that they have the courage to ask you questions that will test your thinking without killing your idea and spirit.

As for those challenging negative people in your life, you don't need to convince yourself that they are wrong, or put them down. You merely need to minimise your exposure to them. Wish them well, say to them inwardly, 'Namaste' and look for all of the wonderful evidence that your approach to success is working.
Secrets of Success 15: THERE IS NO SUCH THING AS A COINCIDENCE will help to show you that it is. Firstly, we'll go to Vhairi

and find out how she has been getting on with people with a problem for every solutions.

Test Drive 14

Funny that Jenny should mention Pollyanna. It was one of my favourite films as a child, and my family often call me Pollyanna. Pollyanna played 'the Glad Game', which involved finding something to be glad about in every situation. Funnily enough, the game is born out of an unwanted Christmas present, when Pollyanna is hoping for a doll but receives a pair of crutches instead. Her father tells her to look at the good side – 'we didn't need to use them?' There is often a reason to be glad in every situation, and writing in the gratitude diary has really helped me to understand how much I have to be grateful for.

It is incredibly refreshing to be in the company of 'Yes' people, but also when you are not used to it, it is a little unsettling. However, like anything positive, as in the case of Pollyanna, it is contagious. When someone confidently says to you, 'Why not?' the chances are that you probably don't have a very good reason for why not, you just haven't thought about it in that way before.

In Scotland where I am from, people can be very cynical. As a child I was brought up to believe that success and wealth were for other people, and that there may even be something wrong about trying to have too much. This means that it has been difficult for me to find people who play 'the Glad Game,' or 'the Yes Game'. However, as I learn more about energy and I start vibrating a more positive frequency, other 'Yes' people appear, and they recognise me as someone open to it. When I feel this instinctively, I go with it, embrace it and have the courage to talk to the person. That is exactly how it happened with Jenny.

With the opportunity of working on this book, Jenny has also been mentoring me. What is great about a mentoring relationship is that a mentor's purpose is for you to be a success in whatever way you want. They are usually someone who is not invested in your personal life, so they can be objective. It provides an opportunity for you to talk objectively about your life experiences and about your goals and visions. By profession and (if they are any good of course) by nature, they are 'Yes' people.

The great thing about my mentoring relationship with Jenny is that she

162

challenges me, and says: 'What steps have you made to get closer to your dreams, or to be at peace with something that has been upsetting you?'

I have also found that my friends and family have started to connect me with other people that might be able to help me in my journey. Since I started telling people that I wanted to be a writer and get a book published, loads of my friends and family have suggested people I should get in touch with. However nerve-wracking it is, I have taken every opportunity to speak to the people they suggest.

I am not the most confident person, but I can hide my shyness to meet strangers for lunch or to go to a house full of people I don't know to talk to a writer. I am putting myself outside of my comfort zone but I want my goal so much that I am prepared to do that. These are people who have achieved what I am trying to achieve. They have said to themselves, 'Why not me?' so I have to know how they got there.

Meeting Jenny and speaking to her about energy and the Universe made me feel so good that I said to her after a few weeks, 'Jenny, I would meet up with you every week just to talk to you.' As it was, we were working on this book but often we would talk about things as a result and before we knew it, an hour had passed and we had to do some work. So we decided that we would create a space in our lives to dedicate to having these kinds of chats. We both had in mind other people that we thought would like that opportunity and we started a group. We called it EVA (Energy, Vibration and Attraction). We meet once a month for the sole purpose of talking about all of the 'airy fairy stuff' we like but that our immediate friends and family are not that into. The first night we met, we were there for three hours. Finally, we were all around people who allowed us to be ourselves, and with whom we could talk freely.

I have found that self-development is a challenging journey, albeit very worthwhile. I am experiencing a lot of different emotions as I really look at myself, at my life, and at my place in the Universe. Often, I am very unsure of myself and of what I am learning. It really helps me to speak to other people who are experiencing the same thoughts and feelings at EVA.

'Coincidence is God's way of remaining anonymous'

Albert Einstein

Secrets of Success 15: THERE IS NO SUCH THING AS COINCIDENCE

Consider the complexity of events that have to align in order for the simplest of things to happen in nature, such as:

- A flower opening its petals.
- A baby being born.
- A raindrop to fall.
- Grass growing

Nature is highly intelligent and extremely organised. Nothing happens by accident. So it is amusing that we think that events that bring two strangers together to make the miracle of life happen, are mere coincidences.

I have a very dear friend who wanted a new job. She went to London for an interview, but the job did not meet her vision. On the way down, she sat next to a man and got chatting to him. She told him why she was going to London and the type of job she would ideally like. 'By coincidence' he knew, through a colleague, of a job that matched her brief almost to the letter, he introduced her to the colleague and subsequently she joined his company several months later. Now is that a coincidence or is it something called synchronicity?

You could see it as a bit of both, unless you look at coincidences as coordinated incidents. When you look at it in that way, you start to see the miraculous magic of life playing out before us.

I have many personal examples, and hundreds of examples of clients with whom I have worked where a clear vision followed by action resulted in 'magical manifestations'. The process is always the same. Had my job-seeking friend not had the ability and the confidence to say loud and clear: 'This is what I want. This is my order,' she may not have been able to make the most of the chance meeting she had on the plane. In fact, I believe that because she had already placed her order before getting on the plane, it was Chef who arranged the seating arrangements on the flight that day to offer up an opportunity.

There are three levels of what I call placing your order or **ASKING:**

- Level 1: Personal vision – taking time to think or dream, and to hold a vision of your life in the future as you wish it.
- Level 2: Daily plans – taking time to plan the events of the day and how you want them to work out.
- Level 3: In-the-moment requests – remembering to take time to ask or to positively pre-script in the moment.

At each level, it does not matter whether your order is large or small. What will make a difference is how aware you are of the signs that it is unfolding, or that an opportunity is presenting itself to you. And then, how open you are to see and celebrate the manifestation when it appears.

You can now finalise your Level 1 vision. Refer back to your draft vision in **Secrets of Success 5: IF YOU WANT TO PREDICT YOUR FUTURE, CREATE IT.** Read it again and consider how you want to enrich it. Rewrite it here and ensure it is full of positive energy and words like: wonderful, exciting, beautiful, easily, enjoyable.

Exercise 14: My Vision

I am so happy and grateful now that I …

Thank you Universe.

Test Drive 15

Like Jenny, when I read and understood what had to happen in order for human beings to exist in Brian Cox's wonderful book, *Human Universe*, I was completely amazed. If you could fully comprehend all of the factors involved in firstly, the creation of our habitable, oxygen-rich planet with its unique solar system; and secondly the billions of years of different conditions that it experienced before life formed; and thirdly, how intelligent life formed (that means us) you can't help but think there is no way these could be coincidences. I understand how you can believe in science and not believe that a God created the Universe but believing that it is all just an accident is equally ridiculous to me.

I believe the same thing about life. None of it is a coincidence. When I started thinking about energy, synchronicity started to occur. When it happens to you, it always gives you a bit of a thrill, because you tap into an understanding that there is something other than you at work here. Now when I say that, I don't necessarily even mean that it is God (but I am humble enough to say that I have no superior knowledge to say that it is not). It could equally be that in order to survive, human beings - like ants for example - are able to communicate with each other, and to the earth, and the things in it in ways that do not involve speech or writing. When you think about it, our brain's main function is to send out messages. Yes, it primarily sends them to our own nervous system, but it makes absolute sense to me that it also sends out signals to other people and things.

Even when I am writing, I go back to stories or novels that I wrote and then never did anything with, and find material for the books and stories I am working on now. Sometimes I think, 'that was the whole point of that story – to fit that little segment into this one'.

The way you meet people is very similar. There are people I have met about whom I thought after various events, 'life may have been better had I not met that person'. But then I think of other people that I may not have met otherwise and I realise that I wouldn't go back and change anything if it meant missing out on this person or that, some of whom have ended up being really important parts of my life.

There are also people that I am completely drawn to. I have connections with several people that I can't explain. They are definitely spiritual connections, and something happens when I talk to these people – they always give me a better understanding of myself and of life. They in turn also seem drawn to me. You hear people say jokingly, 'I am sure I knew you in a previous life.' But honestly, I think we have met these people before. Some spiritual philosophies believe that we choose the people we have in our lives before we are born, including the people we don't like, based on what it is we want to learn in this life. For me, any of this is possible.

Every time I think about where I am in life right now and who is in it, absolutely everything that ever happened - big or small, good or bad - had to happen to bring me right to this spot. And I like the spot I am in better and better as I go along, so I wouldn't go back and change anything. I truly understand that none of it was a coincidence.

My Vision reloaded

I am so happy and grateful now that so many opportunities have started to come my way for writing. I am able to write about things that I have a huge interest in, and therefore it comes so easily to me. People cannot help but react positively to my writing because it is genuine and unique. I am finding writing and working on my creative projects, easy, flowing and fun. I truly feel like I am doing exactly what I should be doing. When my fingers touch the keyboard, they flow freely.

It is so amazing that we have got DTS published and it is selling! We are making money from it - it is such a great achievement. I am so proud of the work we have put into it and how it has turned out. Jenny and I are spreading a loving, winning and inspiring energy around everyone we come across with our book. Millions of people are reading it, getting involved and starting or continuing their journeys of self-development. We are so happy to see people inspired.

It is really wonderful to feel the support and encouragement I am getting and to see all of the people I am inspiring and encouraging to live life the way they want to. I feel like I am making a difference to other people's lives.

I have finished *Miss Jane* and shared it with lots of my friends and people who have helped me to make it the best it can be. It is exciting, thrilling and empowering for women. Women are inspired to be the hero when they read it and guys love the character of Miss Jane.

All of the hard work I have put in over the last few years is really paying off. I am focused, determined, energised and clear about what I want and what I need to do to get it. I do not worry about having enough money, I am having so much fun donating it, giving it to the people I love, and spending it on trips travelling around the world.

I am staying in a beautiful home that I love with a huge gorgeous garden, feeling like I belong here. I can easily afford to stay here and I have plenty of cash flow for all of the things I need and all of the things I want. I am happy that this is a permanent base. I hold parties and gatherings here; my home is a hub of people and ideas. It vibrates a great energy. I have a room with a gorgeous view for writing. It has been great fun decorating it and filling it with unique, antique, funky furniture.

I am so pleased that I figured out how to love openly, freely and without expectation. I am confident that I am worthy of love. I have a partner who I can love freely, lightly and whom I have great fun and adventures with. We laugh a lot together. I can talk to him about everything – he accepts everything about me, all of my vices and quirks. I love him in the same way. He is strong, healthy and fit. He is interested in things I am interested in. We can talk about the Universe and energy and he thinks I am smart and lovely and beautiful.

My parents, my sister and her husband and their children visit, my neighbours, and lots of friends and family, and all of the lovely women I have met in my life who have helped me are around. I have a cat. It is peaceful. The sun is shining. I am sitting with my partner beside me, his arm around me, quiet and content. We often have my friends from other countries and their families here staying with us.

I am doing more and more good charitable work around the world. I know that the little things I do make a difference. I am an inspiration. I am showing everyone around me that you can achieve anything you want if you believe it. I am a living example of how a woman can be a woman and can be vulnerable and feminine as well as intelligent, sexy and confident.

I am one-by-one ticking off everything on my bucket list. Visiting all of the places I want to see. I am in a state of wonder about the beauty of the world around me. I truly appreciate it, and how special it is to experience it in this way.

I really feel like I understand what I need to do to keep myself happy and peaceful. It is easy to do all of the things that keep me happy, focused and energised. I have never felt so healthy or so full of positive energy. I have improved concentration, memory, focus, understanding and compassion from my yoga practices. It helps me in everything I do. I do yoga every day, and can do it anywhere at any time. I have created a diet that suits me and keeps me energised and healthy. It is easy to stick to it because I love healthy, delicious food.

I genuinely believe in myself and my capabilities. I feel older, wiser, bolder, braver and altogether stronger within myself. I am completely at ease with myself and I accept every part of myself and every feeling I have – high and low. I understand that this is what the experience of life is. I am learning to be detached from these feelings, and to my feelings about other people, meaning I can love everything and everyone freely and without expectation.

I truly understand that it can be the best fun ever if you just play life like you are playing a beautiful piece of music. People are drawn to me in the way butterflies are drawn to flowers – they come and they go and they spread the seeds everywhere. The more I let go of, the more things come to me.

Thank you Universe.

'It is our choices … that show what we truly are, far more than our abilities.'

J. K. Rowling

Secrets of Success 16: LIFE IS A SERIES OF CHOICES

The beauty of being successful at **doing** something is that you get to decide what you do. Now I sense that a good many readers will scoff at that statement and say: 'It's alright for you, you're rich or you've got your own business, you can choose. That's not possible for me, I am stuck in a boring job, or an unfulfilling relationship, or I have too many commitments'. Well if you are currently doing a job that doesn't make you happy or are in an unfulfilling relationship, I would still challenge you to say that you do have a choice.

Many years ago, when I was left alone to bring up my first son, I thought I was trapped and had no choice but to return to work to pay the mortgage. I resented my situation and berated my ex-husband for putting me in the situation. He, at the time, had a fixed view of the contribution he was willing to make to support his child. I now know that I was doing several very unhelpful things.

Firstly, I was blaming him for my current situation and not taking responsibility for the earlier choices I had made that had resulted in my current life scenario. Secondly, my focus was on my feelings of frustration and disappointment. And remember: **WHAT YOU PUT YOUR FOCUS ON IS WHAT YOU GET.**

In essence I was thinking and behaving like a victim not a victor. And I had lots of people who were happy to support me in that analysis of the situation, effectively keeping me there. Remember: always be wary of well-meaning friends.

When I realised that I was feeding my own depression, I sat down and had a firm chat with myself. Did I really have no choice about my situation? I realised that actually I had many choices available to me even if initially they seemed to be totally unacceptable. I seriously considered the following choices:

    a. I could give up work and claim benefits. This would probably mean I would have to sell my house, move to a council flat (assuming I would get one), give up my company car, give up our holidays and not be able to send my son to a good nursery for his early development.

    b. I could give up my job, move in with my Dad, and give up my freedom and privacy.

c. I could go part-time and just about hold onto the house but give up all other aspects of my life.

d. I could remain working and continue with my life as it was and accept I would need to continue to rely on people to help me.

e. I could possibly retrain and become a child-minder, stay at home with my son and keep my house.

Faced with so many options and possibilities I was now in a position to choose the one that I believed would work best for my son and for me. I decided to continue to work at the job I loved. I reached out and asked for help from my father and mother in-law, which they were only too happy to give me, and I established a strong paid-for support network of child care and home help which enabled me to spend all of my available time with my son. My thinking and focus had shifted from blame and shame to choice and rejoice. In being able to choose I was taking responsibility for my decision.

In the years that followed, if ever I got downhearted I would remind myself that I do have a choice and that this was my choice. In the light of new information or changing circumstances, I always had the opportunity to choose again, rejoicing in the freedom of an abundance of possibilities and the mystery of the journey of life.

You see, one of the things that separates us from animals is that we have the ability to choose. We can change our direction and destiny and not be driven solely by our primal instincts. We may not like some of the options or alternatives available to us but we can choose so always remember - **LIFE IS A SERIES OF CHOICES.**

In time, I also learnt that when we free ourselves from the conditioning of society, which has us believing things like: 'I could never do that. Not being employed means I am a failure. I need x, y and z to survive,' we become free to see choices as wonderful opportunities and unlimited possibilities instead of penalties for failure or poor judgement or planning. In fact, we are giving ourselves the choice to adopt a whole new set of behaviours, which is golden nugget, **Secrets of Success 17: CHOOSE TO BE A VICTOR NOT A VICTIM.** But first, what choices has Vhairi made?

Test Drive 16

When I moved into my first flat with my friend, I remember actually feeling quite overwhelmed about the fact that I could choose everything myself, without interference, advice or suggestions. I would literally walk around the flat thinking, 'Should I do that? Ooh, actually, I can do whatever I want.' Of all of the things I have learned, the most liberating one is that I have a choice in everything. When you first start to learn about energy and about the law of attraction, it is an incredible discovery.

It is perfectly easy to coast along for an entire lifetime thinking that life is something that just happens to you. When I started learning about energy, and reading books like Christine McGrory's *Grace* and Louise Hay's *Affirmations to Heal Your Life*, I realised that all along I had been making choices, and it was very clear to me that I had been making all of the wrong choices. The truth is, I was a follower. I did what other people were doing because I was scared to do things on my own, and I was scared to let people down in case they wouldn't like me any more if I didn't.

Like Jenny, I was very much behaving like a victim. I blamed other people and society for the situation I was in, and therefore I believed that the path I was on was inevitable. I even believed that certain things about my personality were in my genes and that there was no way of escaping them. I do believe certain things are in your genes, but I now also believe that you can change even the circuitry of your brain over time. I am absolutely certain I have changed mine. I think there is undoubtedly something about our genes that can make us prone to depression, anxiety and addiction. You can understand and acknowledge that instead of believing that you are destined for a life of addiction (legal or illegal). My experience is that you will have to work a little harder to find good ways to offset that imbalance, but that it's absolutely possible to do that.

The hormonal imbalance I experience every other month (it must only be one ovary that's depressed) means that I lose hope. I can't find hope in anything that I do. But because I have looked at this, I know what it is and I know that it will pass. I let it be and I continue. Whether my heart is in it or not, I continue to do the vibration management routine, and as many of the things I am working on as possible. I am much gentler with myself and I tell myself it is ok just to sit about and think about things for a while. I still have choices about what to do about it. I choose not to drink or take drugs. I choose not to try and escape it. I choose to do exercise regularly, I choose to do yoga and meditate, I choose to speak to people I know will understand, I choose to write, to read and sometimes just to lie in my bed listening to music.

Everything I have learned through meditation has taught me that the best thing is not to judge these feelings. It is not to say that they are wrong and should be avoided at all costs, or that I should pretend they are not there, but instead to look at how I feel without judgement and accept that this is a part of my human experience.

There is the possibility for good to come out of everything. I believe that my hormonal depression allows me to feel a greater degree of compassion for other people, and it enables me to have much more understanding. It means I am able to be more kind and comforting with people who are suffering from these types of feelings.

When I am feeling these things, I let the things in my head all run out into my writing and that feels good. Sometimes things need to be said. Sometimes I need to look at some of the things I am doing and say to myself: 'Hmm. I shouldn't have done that. I actually really didn't like the way that made me feel. I am not sure if I am spending my time in the right way. Do I really want the things I say I want?' These are important questions that I really should be asking myself regularly.

Jenny's previous analogy about a car's warning system is so right – if a light is turned on you have to investigate the root of the problem – you can't just turn it off or pretend it is not on.

This liberating feeling I had when I moved into my first flat has stayed with me throughout. The truth is, I make a lot of choices that other people around me wouldn't. I have chosen a different way of life than the societal norm where I live. I have chosen not to settle down, buy a house and raise a family. I have chosen instead to spend my time, money and energy on chasing my dreams. I am actively attempting to put into place doing everything I would like to do. This means that I am constantly questioned about my choices. Like people questioning whether I should rent or buy a house. Like people asking why I am going on a trip to Thailand on my own. Like people asking why I don't have a boyfriend.

I choose to be different because I have a load of things I just have to do first. I have ended up in this unique position where I have very few responsibilities, I am earning a decent amount of money, I have created time and space in my life to work on creative projects, and I am surrounding myself with people and information that is helping me to believe that I can do anything. Why do I do these things? It is because they make me feel good. It doesn't mean that my choices are better than anyone else's – some people feel really good when they feel secure. Families feel a wonderful sense of joy when they are together and are expressing their love for one another. But it is not the only way to feel joy and peace. I feel a wonderful sense of joy when I am walking in the hills on my own, or when I am at the beach writing.

Some people will say I am weird, or kooky or crazy, but I learned the hard way that if I don't focus my energy on doing the things I like because I think I should be doing the things everyone else is doing, I become deeply unhappy and life feels pointless, boring and sad to me.

I always know when I am doing something that is really right for me. When I have been travelling in the past, I have had wonderful little moments where I feel like everything is exactly as it should be. I am in exactly the right place, doing the right thing – and in fact so is everyone else. These amazing little moments convince me that I am on the right track.

I have to take a lot of risks to do these things, like spend money on trips instead of saving for a deposit for a house in the belief that one day I will make enough money to buy my own house. Like having uncomfortable conversations with people to ask if I can do things. I have to put my fears to the side when I jump on a plane to the other side of the world entirely on my own. But I always have a choice. And although I often think to myself, 'Bollocks. How did I get myself into this one?' I know that being scared is not a good enough reason not to do something.

'Your victory is right around the corner. Never give up.'

Nicki Minaj

Secrets of Success 17: CHOOSE TO BE A VICTOR NOT A VICTIM!

In the previous scenario where I had a big life decision to make, I had chosen to be a victor not a victim. Now, take a few minutes to think about what it feels like to be a victim. Let your shoulders sag and your head drop down, feel the sadness and anxiety. It really doesn't feel good and you would probably like to hide in a corner.

Now think about how it feels to be victorious. Imagine a feeling of excitement and adrenalin coursing through your veins. Your head held high, pulse racing, flushed with the glow of satisfaction. Your confidence is high and you are ready to face the world.

I know which one I would like to experience and that is why I choose victory every time. There have been many situations where life has dealt me unfavourable hands, but by following the choice principle I always ensure I am clear that I am not a victim of circumstance but a victor in the face of adversity.

You too can choose victory. All you need to do is follow these simple steps:

1. Recognise when you are listening to the 'I have no choice' inner voice.
2. Sit down and write down the choices you do have. Even though many of them are uncomfortable or not acceptable, they are still choices available to you. Only by looking at them carefully and really challenging yourself as to why they are not acceptable choices to you (they may be perfectly acceptable to someone else) will you be able to seriously discount them. You may even shock yourself by taking one of them!
3. Adopt the body language of a victor. Head held high, smile on your face, deep breaths. Your subconscious will think you are already a victor and help you to choose the best option for yourself.
4. Select the 'best' option from your list and start to do all you can to implement it.
5. Congratulate yourself on being a victor and remind yourself often that you do have a choice.
6. Be proud of your choice and enjoy it.

You may find that you feel like you have to accept a choice because of some limitation that you may have. Maybe you lack qualifications that would allow you to change your job or maybe you are living in the wrong place. If, having gone through this process, you realise you want to make changes in your life then the next exercise will help you. All you have to do is follow the headings on each section. I have completed the first one as an example for you.

This exercise is for addressing known areas for improvement and uses **Secrets Of Success 3 and 5: WHAT YOU PUT YOUR FOCUS ON IS WHAT YOU GET** and: **IF YOU WANT TO PREDICT YOUR FUTURE CREATE IT**.

Don't forget to transfer the actions you have come up with into your diary or scheduler. By doing so, and actually following through, you will soon be enjoying even more success at doing something.

Exercise 15: Life Improvement Action Plan

Action Plan Area:	Date:
Where I am now:	
Where I want to be in 12 months' time	
Where I want to be in 3 months' time	
How I will get there (specific actions)	

Action Plan: Jenny Copeland	Age: 47	
Area: Health		Date:
Where I am now: • Unhappy at being 2 stone overweight • Talking regular gentle exercise but no cardio vascular workouts • Suffering from migraines (gradually getting worse)		Jan 07
Where I want to be in 12 months' time • At least 1 stone lighter and happy with my continual weight loss • Still walking the dog regularly • Doing an intensive workout 3 times a week • In control if not free from migraines		Jan 08
Where I want to be in 3 months' time • Half a stone lighter and losing on average 1lb a week • Doing 8000 steps a day through regular daily dog walks • Doing an intensive workout 3 times a week • Having seen the doctor experiencing an improvement in the frequency of my migraines		March 07
How I will get there (specific actions) • Plan my eating programme a week in advance and shop for the right ingredients weekly • Take healthy packed lunches to work daily • Walk dog daily • Have healthy emergency standby snacks in my handbag • Get fitness buddies and commit to an exercise plan • Book an appointment with the doctor		3.2.07 5.2.07 Daily Daily 4.2.07 6.2.07

Test Drive 17

This chapter is very relevant for me right now. I stay in a lovely home that I love, but I rent a home from someone who is planning on selling it. I really love the home, and feel very happy here. In truth, I don't want to leave it. At the moment, I am trying to convince myself that I do have a choice, and it has become a huge drive to obtain some success with my writing. If I can get a book published and it is a big seller, I could buy my house. (written in May 2016)

Test Drive Exercise 15: Life Improvement Action Plan

Area	Date
Where I am now: Staying in a beautiful home that I love with a huge gorgeous garden, sharing with people I like, feeling like I belong here. I can easily afford to stay here and have plenty of cash flow for all of the things I need and many of the things I want. The home is not mine, and there is the possibility that I will be told to move in the next few months. The house is not being kept the way it should be. I can't afford to buy the house, but the opportunity to do so is there. I have just started working 1.5 days from home on my creative projects and my virtual PA work. I have up to 12 hours a week work virtual PA work. I have several creative projects on the go that will have a financial return eventually, but I am not making money from writing or creative projects. I have enough extra income from my virtual PA client, and for the next few months, will most likely have enough work. I am working out 5 times a week, doing circuits, running, walking and yoga. The weather has been so nice we have been working out at the beach and I have done yoga in the back garden. I ran 8 miles yesterday and am considering doing a	31/5/16

marathon in October. I am very nearly at my goal of a 26-inch waist (26 if I breathe in). I feel more energised than I have in a very long time. I am honestly happy with the figure I have and the way I look. I understand how blessed I am to feel that way. I can do a headstand, but I can't hold it for very long. I can do a press up on my toes.

I am single, but I am open to dating people, and have even instigated some dates myself. I have several men in my life whom I enjoy being around, but I am not in a relationship with anyone. I am enjoying my life, but I would like to meet a partner.

Where I want to be in 12 months' time

I am staying in a beautiful home that I love with a huge gorgeous garden, feeling like I belong here. I can easily afford to stay here and I have plenty of cash flow for all of the things I need and all of the things I want. I am happy that this is a safe base. My home is a hub of people and ideas. It vibrates a great energy. I work from home and I am incredibly happy with the choices I have made.

I am proud of the way I took the situation with both hands and steered it with the help of people around me. I am truly grateful to everyone who helped me to get here. I can afford the upkeep of the house and garden, and to do some redecorating and upgrading. It feels like a real achievement to have arranged it so that I am the custodian of a wonderful part of the world.

I have completed the projects I was working on at the beginning of the year, one of which has been successful and is now earning income. I am regularly paid to write film reviews on a freelance basis. I am also being paid for other writing. One of my stories has been bought and is being made into a film adaptation.

I am incredibly proud of the work I am producing because I feel like I am playing. I love doing the work I am doing so much, it doesn't feel like work at all, and because I have such wonderful energy when I am doing it, other people feel that and love it too.

I have a 26-inch waist, I feel fit, strong and energised. I am physically active every day. I have done a yoga teacher training course and can now comfortably do a headstand, hold it and do some variations. I am now doing yoga classes as an extra income.

I am in a relationship with someone who is easy and loving and supportive. They are fun to be around and encourage me to take fun risks. It feels easy and fun and light.

Where I want to be in 3 months' time

Staying in a beautiful home that I love with a huge gorgeous garden, sharing with people I like, feeling like I belong here. I can easily afford to stay here and have plenty of cash flow for all of the things I need and many of the things I want. I know where I am going to be staying next year, and have a plan in place for that to happen.

I have started to receive income for writing. I have planned an awesome holiday at the end of the Summer where I will see some friends I have been missing, to places I have never been.

How I will get there (specific actions)

Ask the Universe for £300,000 to buy this house daily.
Enter writing competitions to try and raise the money.
Look out for opportunities to raise the money or to stay in this house. Ask any prospective buyers if they would be willing to rent my room to me.

To stay in another house, ask around and look for another room to rent.

Work Finish Drive-Thru Success and pitch to publishers Finish journal and exercises for Drive-Thru Success Subscribe to Total Film and contact them about writing for them Draft pitches and send to magazines and newspapers Send more short stories to competitions and publications Finish Miss Jane **Virtual PA** Create a mailshot and send to list of contacts from Business Gateway Go to Business Gateway courses Update website and renew subscription	

When I wrote my vision above in May 2016, I wanted to stay in the house I was living in and actually several opportunities came up that could have allowed me to buy the house. One was to take over the mortgage and expenses and rent out the rooms to other people. I decided that although that did answer my wish, there were reasons that I didn't want to do that, largely to do with my peace of mind.

In April 2017, I had been staying in a flat at the seaside for 6 months. It was a lovely flat with plenty of space. I could absolutely afford to stay there and do all of the things I wanted. It didn't have a huge gorgeous garden, unless you count the seashore two minutes from my house. However, I had been thinking for some time about how I liked staying there, but I really wished I had a flat with a sea view. I was having one of my wobbles and was saying (as I sometimes do), 'Come on Universe, give me a sign, let me know what you're up to, I'm not getting it right now. I am working hard and things are not coming. Help me out mate.' We received a notice to leave the flat the next day. I could have been upset about this, but instead I saw it as a sign, and as the Universe answering me. It's now July 2017 and I have moved into a flat directly across the road. As I sit updating my input into this chapter, I am looking out of my window at the view of the sea I have from my bed.

The vision of owning my own house with a huge gorgeous garden is still in my head, in my affirmations and on my vision board. And I believe that I will absolutely achieve it. I do also understand that this is a big **ASK** and that I haven't put in enough work for it yet, and that is ok.

At times I am very impatient with this process, like the other night when I was thinking that the things I am asking for are not coming. Luckily I have Jenny to remind me that your **ASKs** can sometimes take time - especially the big ones.

I went to Thailand for 4 weeks and had a wonderful time on a yoga teacher-training course in a beautiful location with lots of amazing similar-minded yogis. I am feeling strong and fit, and I am able to stay in a headstand for 5 minutes. The headstand has come off, and a scorpion is now on my vision board. Yoga teacher training was also on it, and it is the first really big thing that I have achieved from my vision board. I was close to not appreciating how this is a direct manifestation of my vision.

I had a conversation with Jenny before I moved out of my house, when I was feeling disheartened and I said to her, 'Yeah but booking the yoga course was easy'. I have thought about that comment a lot recently. There would have been a time when it would have seemed impossible, and it is a true reflection of how far I have come in myself and in my life for me to feel that it was easy. A lot of things lined up for that to be possible. So many different things – from someone being off at work all summer and my taking the decision not to take a holiday until she returned, to my asking for most of the time off for a travel writing competition that I did not win, to my boss turning up one day unexpectedly when I was thinking about whether I should ask her about it, to my receiving a tax rebate that allowed me to pay for it. It was only easy because the Universe stacked all of these things up in a row for me.

'Belief is a wise wager. Granted that faith cannot be proved, what harm will come to you if you gamble on its truth and it proves false?

If you gain, you gain all; if you lose, you lose nothing. Wager, then, without hesitation, that He exists.'

Blaise Pascal

Secrets of Success 18: IF YOU THINK YOU CAN OR YOU THINK YOU CAN'T THEN YOU ARE RIGHT: SUCCESS AT HAVING THINGS

I would like to share a few of my thoughts regarding having things.

Firstly, I believe that there is absolutely nothing wrong with wanting or having things. I continuously refer to the abundance all around us and feel that it should be shared with everyone. I do not believe that poverty in itself makes poor people or the 'have not's" any godlier or somehow spiritually superior than rich people or the 'haves'. I do, however, think that the modern pursuit of stuff to make us feel good is unhealthy. Our behaviour is being driven by our senses as they are manipulated by advertising. We are hypnotised into believing that we need stuff and that by having it, it will satisfy our emotional needs.

Many of us are trapped in a cycle of spending 'because we're worth it!' and debt because 'for everything else there is MasterCard.' Debt has been dressed up with so many fancy names, such as easy payment terms, buy now pay later, extended credit, and interest free credit, that we often we don't even acknowledge that it is debt.

I always encourage people to focus on what they want in every aspect of their lives emotionally, spiritually, physically and materially and later on I will be encouraging you to want anything your heart desires. I will tell you not to worry about the cost but I will tell you not to get into debt in order to have those things. If you truly want something and it is good for you, the Universe will find a way to get it to you – without the use of VISA.

I have experienced chronic debt and all the misery associated with it. If you are in debt, get help now. It is important that you feel like you have earned everything you have – either by working for it, or by being a generous person who is open to giving and receiving continuously. When everything you give and receive is done with love and a feeling of generosity, it is a light, free-flowing process. Debt can be a heavy load to carry because you may not feel like you have earned it, and also because of its associations with a lot of negative vibrations. It becomes something you want rid of and that you find it difficult to face. There are times when in this

190

day and age it may be necessary, but always have the intention of paying it off and understand that it is a temporary solution and not a way of life.

If you are not in debt, commit now never to go there. Why? **Because it's not worth it**

This principle also impacts on your decision to go for things like jobs, relationships, holidays or that outfit. How often have you talked yourself out of something because you have decided you won't or can't? This is simply a thought and thoughts can be changed.

So decide now that you can and you will.

Take the first step confident that whatever you are going for is one more action away. So yes you can!

Test Drive 18

I read a quote from Dr Wayne Dyer recently, 'Abundance is not something we acquire. It is something we tune into.'

This is a very new way to look at money for me. I was born and raised in the West of Scotland with a professional mother and a working class father. We were somewhat in the middle of those two classes. I am not aware of my parents' getting into heavy debt, but they had to use it for some things. I still developed a very unhealthy hatred for money. I saw how it can really stress people out and make them feel like they are not worthy if they don't have enough. I also believed that it made all people greedy and selfish and that it was the root of evil in this world.

When I look back now, I see that I was focusing a lot of negative energy on money, and therefore, I always seemed to be chasing my tail. I didn't believe that I would ever earn a lot of money. I thought being rich was for other people and although I always had faith that I would have enough – I believe I am a hard worker, and willing to take on any job - I never believed that I would be anything other than working class. There is absolutely nothing wrong with being working class, or not wanting to have any more than that. But there absolutely is something wrong with thinking that it is not your choice and that there is nothing you could do about it, or that it is selfish or greedy.

My parents could not have afforded tuition fees, so to go to University I had to get student loans. I was also offered an overdraft that I increased every month because I kept spending more money. I worked since I was 15, and when I was at University, at one point I had 3 jobs. I was earning money, but I was spending more of it than I was earning. When I finished University, I was quite downhearted – I had a huge overdraft that was no longer free and had to take out a bank loan to pay it off, and I had a student loan (which, thankfully due to the Scottish Government I didn't have to pay until I earned more money). I also started using credit cards and juggled a little with that. I got a lot of bank charges for missed payments, going over my overdraft and was paying a lot of interest. It was not a good place to be in.

I only ever looked at my bank statement on pay day, and at the end of the month, would play bank machine bingo and just put the card in and see if it would let me withdraw anything.

I decided that I was fed up with having debt – at the time this was largely because I was angry with myself for paying credit card companies and banks a whole load of unnecessary money. They were greedy and selfish, but I was enabling them to be that way. I made a decision to pay everything off and become debt-free, and when I came home from Australia, I managed to not owe a single penny to anyone. It was a good feeling.

There are also times when it is sensible – as long as you are sensible about it. When I came home and went to buy my first car, I bought a car with cash. I decided I would not be like everyone else, and I would do it the old-fashioned way. I now refer to that car as the bad egg. It was a terrible purchase – through a friend's ex-boyfriend who bought it on eBay. It was supposed to have a new gearbox fitted, but it didn't and the gearbox was knackered. It was incredibly stressful to drive, and I spent a few hundred quid on it before I was told it would need a whole new gearbox that was worth more than the car itself. I decided to buy a newer car, because the stress and unhappiness of driving a car that did not work was not worth it for me. I wanted peace of mind and to enjoy driving a car, and I was willing to pay for that. So I got a loan and bought a relatively new car and my new car became the good egg.

Because the way I look at everything has changed, the way I look at having things has also changed. There is, as Jenny says, nothing wrong with having things. You only cause yourself unhappiness if you covet things, if you have attachment to things, or if you buy things for status symbols or prestige.

Most things have a purpose. My car has a purpose – to allow me to get to places quickly, safely and easily – and I don't need to drive a Jaguar to do that. Clothes are necessary to keep me warm and to cover up my body – but they can also be an expression of who I am as a person. I don't think there is anything wrong with that either and I love clothes. If I see something and I love it, I buy it. I buy it because I feel good wearing it, and when I feel good wearing something, my vibrations are positive and that helps me to go through life happily. I shop in charity stores and accept other people's hand-

193

me-downs if I like them. I have no snobbery about it. I also give all of my used good clothes to charity shops.

I now look at my bank account regularly, and I budget. It helps me to have an idea of how much I can spend throughout the month without getting into debt. I do sometimes buy things on a credit card, but always with the intention of paying it back – and if I have the money, I will pay in cash for anything first.

I read that a good way to look at things is that we never truly own anything forever – we are merely custodians of things, we are looking after them. Money is not something you collect – it is something you use to trade. We have sadly forgotten that it had a very simple purpose when it was created.

I listened to a lecture by Alan Watts in which he said that often people go to the supermarket and think of all of the money they are spending and are loath to hand it over... making it a negative experience, when really they should be thinking proudly of the work they have done to earn money to buy all of these delicious food and drink products. I often remind myself of this when I am shopping. I look at the food I have and think about how lucky I am that I can afford it. Nearly every day in my gratitude diary, I give my thanks for all of the delicious food and drink I have had – thinking of all of the people around the world who are starving and would love to eat even a small portion of the luxurious food I am fortunate enough to be able to afford.

As soon as I changed my perspective on money, I started to be able to afford things that seemed impossible before. Money seems to come in unexpected ways. I try to look at my bank account positively and appreciate all of the hard work I have put in to earn the money I am earning. I feel this even more for my freelance work. It is actually really good fun counting it up and seeing it grow in my bank account.

It has taken me a long time to convince myself that it is ok to want things and to want to be wealthy... as long as I do it freely with love.

'All you need in this life is ignorance and confidence, and then success is sure.'

Mark Twain

Secrets of Success 19: 'WEEBLES WOBBLE BUT THEY DON'T FALL DOWN'

This Universe we reside in is a living ecosystem that continuously seeks to renew itself through regeneration. Part of this process demands endings. The Universe in essence expands and contracts, a bit like breathing, and all things go through cycles of change.

The sea is in perpetual motion with tides coming in and going out. Plant life exists in cycles of growth: the shoot comes, then the stem, then the branch, the leaf, the bud, the flower, and the fruit, only to start all over again.

Animals are born and die: some choose a complex journey from caterpillar to pupa to chrysalis to butterfly; and others, likes snakes, shed their skin completely to regenerate themselves. Our lives, too, consist of a journey of many experiences and conditions. We experience good and difficult times, happy and sad times, health and illness. Sometimes it is only through this contrast that we truly appreciate what we have. There are so many extremely rich people who are unhappy and many people living very simple lives who are totally fulfilled.

I have learnt that following the **20 Secrets of Success** principles on a daily basis is the best way to thoroughly enjoy the good times and get through the difficult times. I have also learnt that it is when times are hard or challenging that we need the principles the most.

People who follow **Secrets of Success** principles (the universal laws described in this book) know that it is through daily diligence and application that they are able to manifest and enjoy a life of choice. Practiced followers have a calm confidence that is reassuring and soothing. They are able to transcend the ebb and flow of life, and experience the abundance and joy of being safe in the knowledge that whatever goes out will return.

It is when times are good that one's beliefs are tested, and through the most difficult times that faith is tested. We can believe in the principles. We can believe in the Universe, the Higher Power, or God - call it what you will. We can believe that we are powerful beyond measure and it is our light that shines in darkness but we must also learn to have faith - faith that as day follows night and as summer follows spring, good times will follow bad times, happiness will follow sadness and abundance will follow scarcity. It is through our faith that we understand it must come to pass. It is through our faith that we are able to focus on what we have and be grateful for it. Faith will allow us to carry on when all seems lost and faith will help us to focus on our dreams and goals in the knowledge that if we continue to follow the process they too shall come to pass.

I am often asked which of the principles is the most important? If I only have time to follow one or two which ones should I do?

The principles when practiced regularly become habits like brushing your teeth or indeed breathing and as such many of them take no time at all. They may take attention and they may require space in the moment for reflection. For example, taking a few seconds to ask yourself: Is this the best thought I can have? Is this belief true? Does it serve me? What am I putting my focus on in this moment? Would I like to change that focus? These things do not take time as such.

If time is limited for the habits and exercises, the one life habit that will have the biggest impact on your success is the daily gratitude routine. From experience it is also the one thing that must be adhered to everyday. I have in the past become complacent about this routine. At times, I have allowed myself to be sloppy and have not done the full routine and sooner or later I notice that I am no longer experiencing the joy and miracles in my life that I was before.

So if time is limited please ensure you maintain your daily gratitude routine, it is without doubt the difference that makes the difference. It will allow you to build your resilience muscle and to underpin and sustain your daily well being, happiness and manifestation abilities.

Test Drive 19

I have to say, that I am very prone to a wobble. I like the fact that I am the type of person who questions everything, but that also means that at times I question all of the things I have learned about energy, manifestation and spirituality too. I am lucky that I have my mentor, Jenny in my life to talk to when I am wobbling. The first thing she will ask is: 'Have you been doing your vibrational management routine?' A lot of the time, I will answer, 'No, but I couldn't do it because of this, this and this.' And she will look at me in a way that says, 'Well, what do you expect?' At other times, I say yes, but I don't believe myself when I say the affirmations or write down my thanks.

For me, it has taken quite a bit of willpower to stick to the routine. It has been hard to find the time as I mentioned earlier. However, after reading *Think and Go Rich*, as I said earlier, I started getting up at 5am, and I have to say that it does make a difference to my day. Writing in my gratitude diary and pre-scripting is something that works so often, I just can't afford not to do it right now. I have also found a great improvement in my mood when I do Pranayama and meditation first thing.

Planning my day is a great way for me to make sure I am working on the things that are important to me every day. It makes me take the time to work on my creative projects. I love writing lists, but I love to tick them off even more. So particularly when I am working from home, it is great to write what it is I want to achieve in a day. I go through this process however I feel. And that is a challenge in motivation and perseverance that I have been learning.

In essence, I am a wobbler, a squiggly line - imperfect, strange and outside of the box, but I like those things, and I like being that way.

I personally don't think that there will be a day when everything clicks into place, once and for all and everything will be hunky dory. That is not what life is about. And I happen to think it would be rather dull. I think that the ups and downs are challenges and that they help me to learn and to grow. I don't think there is any endpoint to that evolution.

Like the philosopher, Alan Watts' says, 'You're it'. My life is all I have. I ain't getting another one anytime soon. So I think that whatever happens when I die, the best thing I can do is find out how to feel real joy in being alive as often as possible.

I am happiest when I accept who I am, warts and all; when I am conscious about what I am doing and how I am feeling; and when I accept this life as it is. Not as it could be or should be, but as it is now. That doesn't mean I don't still have challenges that help me grow, evolve and better my experience. It doesn't mean I shouldn't be striving towards things – perhaps the end is not what is so enjoyable about the striving, but the act of working towards things. Since I started having goals and visions, I have never been more energised or satisfied.

I count myself as blessed that I am a living reinvention that will never stay the same. There is a huge potential in the fact that I wobble. Every time I do – like when I am trying to hold a difficult yoga balance - I build muscle, I concentrate my mind and I find that if I breathe and calm my mind, I can stay in the position longer than I thought.

The idea of this book is simple – find out what you feel about yourself now, how you would like to feel about yourself, what you need to do to get there and then learn how to stay upright even when you are wobbling.

'When you truly give up trying to be whole through others, you end up receiving what you always wanted from others.'

Shakti Gawain

Step 3: ACTUALISE - COLLECT YOUR ORDER

One beautiful Sunday, (we do have them in Scotland!) my family and I were going to the beach for a picnic. I had made up the picnic full of sandwiches, fruit, cakes, drinks and various goodies and decided that half a dozen bags of chips from a local drive-thru would make the picnic more hearty and warming.

Eventually I managed to load the children, their friends, the dog and the picnic into the car and as usual I was running a few minutes late. People who know me will know that is a mild understatement!

My husband also needed collecting from his local football supporters club, so I dropped him a text saying I would be there in 10 minutes. I looked at my watch and figured I had just enough time to swing by the drive-thru, get the chips, collect my husband and still get to the beach before sunset.

I drove to window one and stated loud and clear: 'Six packets of regular fries please'. I drove to window two and paid the fiver for my order. As I was doing this I received a text message from my husband saying: 'Where are you?'

Somewhat distracted I put my foot down and drove straight to the supporters club. No sooner had I left the drive-thru and my young children were all shouting in their cute Scottish accents: 'We cannae smell the chips mammy!'

Even though I had ordered and paid for them I had managed to drive straight past the collection window!

I share this story because it perfectly illustrates how many people put loads of effort into step 1 and 2 yet still fail to observe and act upon step 3.

I frequently coach people who are clear about what it is they want. They create fabulous action plans and start doing the actions - in essence, paying the price - yet when it comes to collecting their order they somehow either:

- don't recognise their order when it is right under their nose; or
- see it and don't reach out because their old fears and limiting beliefs kick in and prevent them from doing so.

Let's look at the first scenario. If you were in a coffee shop and ordered a coffee but the restaurant only had a teacup:

- Would the coffee taste any different?
- Would you send it back and wait for a coffee cup to become available?
- Would you look into the cup to see if it was indeed coffee?
- Would you clarify that you would have preferred the coffee cup but that you will drink the coffee anyway because that is what you wanted?

Well how often have you asked for a specific kind of relationship and along comes a man or woman who meets 95% of your criteria but maybe the packaging isn't quite what you expected.

Or you have wanted an ideal house or job and one that matches most of your expectations comes along but you would need to move further out than you had hoped.

In any of these situations you have a choice. You can reach out and accept the order and 'taste' it. You can try it on for size. Go along to the interview for the job, go on a date or visit the house and look at the surrounding area. You may surprise yourself and find that this coffee in a teacup is actually better than you had originally hoped for.

Alternatively you can simply say to Chef: 'This isn't quite what I was expecting so I would like to reject it and clarify that X is actually important to me!'

Chef will not judge you, she will merely withdraw her first attempt and go back and start cooking again, factoring in your new refined or clarified requirements.

You can reject Chef's attempts as often as you wish as long as it really is your desire for the ideal that is causing you to reject the offerings and not in fact the second of the two reasons for refusal: **fear and lack of self-belief or confidence.**

Only you will know which is the real reason. If it is the latter then that's ok too. This simply means you have more work to do on your own self-esteem before you are ready to take receipt of your order.

You can either do this by working with a friend or indeed once again you may benefit from getting professional help through a recommended professional such as a coach or counsellor. Indeed your GP may be able to refer you to a counsellor or therapist.

There are many excellent and fast therapies that can help eradicate low self-esteem these days. Nobody need go through life having less that they would want for themselves and you are no exception. If your life isn't all you want it to be and you have followed the exercises and steps in this book and you are still not experiencing improvements, then it really is time to get some additional help. Amongst my extensive toolkit I use some very fast interventions that help people experience super-fast recovery… there are many practitioners like me available, so do some research.

The best and simplest routine to invest in, free of charge, is the **Vibration Management Routine** referred to in chapter 13.

Follow this daily routine and you will notice how easily you can and do manifest. You will also have a track record of all your little successes and how much happier you are day by day.

Vibration Management Routine

First thing in the morning:

- Check in with your emotions. Make a decision there and then about how you want to feel.
- Ensure your first thoughts are those of gratitude. Write down 5 things you are grateful for as you enter your day (feel free to have more than 5).
- Read your vision card and recite the Daily Resetting Your Focus Mantra.
- To-do list – write into your journal the key things that are happening that day and how you want them to work out, also how you want to feel about them.
- If you can possibly find the time, meditate.

Throughout the day:
- Remember to keep asking for every little thing that you want. When you get it remember to say thank you. Always keep your focus on what you want.

Last thing at night:

- Write into your journal at least five things that you are grateful for from that day. This will help you to go to sleep in a really positive frame of mind and will improve the quality of your sleep and help you to wake up refreshed and positive. I call it getting out of the right side of the bed.

Remember:
- Think of what you want.
- Ask for it.
- Let go and trust it will come to you.
- Be ready and open to receive it when it does turn up.
- It may not look exactly as you originally envisioned it.

Dealing with adversity

I think I said right at the beginning of this book that I would share more of my story, and I have. Now, I would like to use the essence of my life story to highlight the **Secrets of Success**, which lend themselves to **dealing with adversity**.

I mentioned earlier that my two brothers and I grew up in the 60s in fairly meagre conditions. Our parents both shared a strong work ethic and did all they could to provide for the family. We started out, the 5 of us in a one-bedroom flat. The 3 children shared the bedroom and mum and dad had half of the living room. A sofa marked the dividing line between their bedroom and our living space.

We were very lucky to have an indoor toilet exclusive to us, and a kitchen with a balcony. A full-sized tin bath lived on the balcony and it was brought into the kitchen weekly for the family bath day. By today's standards this was real hardship but I can still remember my mum stating with pride, 'Of course we have a bath!' I guess back then families were still using public baths. Oh, and I forgot to mention my mum was a raging snob. She had grown up in more favourable circumstances, as she frequently reminded my father, who was from a humble home in a small farming community.

Our parents had limited parenting skills and as was normal then, traditional ideas about discipline, which included 'spare the rod and spoil the child'.

All in all it was a bit like growing up in a pressure cooker - too many bodies in a small space. There was never enough money for luxuries and an underlying, unspoken air of resentment and blame. Resentment that too many children had been born in too short a period of time and both blaming the other for being stuck in noisy, dirty, labouring jobs that paid poorly and demanded long hours.

It was obvious that everybody living in the flat was intelligent and that the route out was through education. My father was determined to see his three children make the most of the opportunity he never had and set about drilling it into us to do well at school and achieve academically. This usually resulted in the three of us being lined up and quizzed quick-fire questions regarding spellings, history, grammar and mathematics. Due to the intense discipline there was always an air of fear attached to these homework review sessions and sadly the fear often contributed to simple forced errors.

My father in his wisdom would then insist on asking us all: 'How stupid are you?' 'Does it hurt to be that stupid?' and 'How can grammar schools produce such stupid children?'

I didn't know anything about self-esteem and self-image at the time. It is only now in retrospect that I can reflect on the damage that this type of behaviour did to all of us. Other mistakes had us labelled bad, dirty and naughty and that is how the three of us viewed ourselves over the years.

The constant repetition of these statements from an authoritarian figure had resulted in our fragile self-images being moulded. This in turn led to me to believe I was stupid, bad, dirty and naughty, and as **Secrets of Success Number 2** states: **I AM WHO I SEE MYSELF TO BE.**

Understanding the relationship between our conscious and subconscious minds is like looking at an iceberg. The bit we see above the water is our conscious self. The massive expanse of ice below the water is our subconscious or self-image or self-esteem.

It is our subconscious beliefs and values that drive our behaviour and it will be no surprise to you to hear that by the time I was 10 I was smoking, by 13 I was drinking, by 14 I was a regular truant and by 15, even, I had given up on myself.

Thankfully alongside all of the negative aspects of my self-image, my parents had also instilled in me a very strong work ethic. I started working when I was 13 and by the time I was 15 I was a chief cashier and supervisor in Tesco responsible for 15 checkouts.

Work became my saviour. We were brought up to be compliant and hardworking and this attitude coupled with my obvious yet not recognised intelligence resulted in a young, willing, enthusiastic employee. Because I received a lot of positive feedback at work, I also developed a very strong self-image there. The more I was told I was viewed as a valued individual, bright and reliable, the more I saw myself in this light and worked to live up to other people's expectations of me.

Now that I fully understand the relationship between my self-image and my behaviour I am very careful to ensure that the person I see myself to be is consistent with the true me. Where I suspect I am holding unhelpful images or beliefs resulting in unhelpful behaviours, I will either use conscious affirmations to address the situation or seek help from a coach or therapist in order to ensure the person I see myself to be is consistent with the true me.

I share this aspect of my story here because I am aware of the disappointment and frustration that can be experienced when you are working with these steps to success and you do not magically achieve as much as the Law of Attraction literature suggests you should.

I have heard myself question the Universe many times, 'Why not me?', 'Am I not good enough?' I have at times allowed myself to become quite anxious and depressed at my lack of manifesting capability.

I now know that this leads to a lower vibration, fear and a magnification of the negative beliefs I hold about myself. This, in turn, leads to less action and at its worst not even doing the most basic daily disciplines. The truth is that I am then in fact manifesting all that I don't want. Directing my energy to my fears and worries and putting my focus on the very things I am trying to avoid or overcome.
I have come to the conclusion that there are ten main reasons why we don't manifest, although I am sure there are more, as I will no doubt find out in the course of my own experiences.

1. Lack of clarity of the request itself.
2. The desire for the **ASK** isn't big enough.
3. Not actually **ASK**ing
4. Lack of belief that we are worthy of our **ASKs**.
5. Lack of **ACTION** towards our **ASKs**.
6. Not being on a manifestation vibration
7. Holding fearful energy regarding the **ASK**.
8. Letting other people talk us out of our **ASKs**.
9. Lack of awareness that our **ASK** has already **ACTUALISED** right in front of us.
10. Not trusting that the Universe has it covered and is working in our best interests.

I have learnt that it is during these times that I need most support and assistance. I need to be gentle with myself and I need to affirm my favourite affirmations:

- **I love myself**
- **I approve of myself**
- **All is well in my world**
- **I am a child of a loving Universe**
- **Everything is exactly as it should be at this moment in time**
- **All is well in my world**

I finish by saying, "Thank you Universe".

The final chapter, **Secrets of Success 20: Supercharge Your Manifesting Muscle with an Attitude of Gratitude,** allows us to cultivate the most helpful and influential habit that virtually guarantees a happier more abundant life.

Test Drive: ACTUALISE

What you might find, like me, is that receiving your **ASK**s is strangely the most challenging out of the 3 steps. It's fine to ASK for things, but how can you receive them if you don't believe you deserve them?

Getting a book published is a great example of the things I go through in my head when I really want something. It involves a lot of hard work and a lot of patience (which I don't always have).

When I want something too much, I squeeze that wish in my hand so tight that it can't get out there into the Universe to do its work and come back to me.

This book has really driven home to me the fact that there is a way to want things: You have to ASK for them, you have to pay your price (usually in sheer hard work), and then you have to let them go, like the wish you make on a dandelion clock. Then you have to recognise that wish when it comes back to you and softly catch it and accept it and know that it was meant for you. Sometimes waiting on that wish coming back can take a long time, but I am developing patience, and I am being kinder and softer about it.

Some people just have to work harder to change the way they think – I am one of those people. Whatever way you look at it, I would never have achieved anything, nor would I have enjoyed achieving anything had I continued to be a pessimist, and that is the crux of it. Where am I as I am writing this? I am sitting in my car on my favourite beach. The sun is shining on the sea and around me is the music of the waves and the birds. Earlier, I went into the café I go to every Sunday, my writing day, and the owner said: 'Ah, it's the writer.'

'As we express our gratitude, we must never forget that the highest appreciation is not to utter words, but to live by them.'

John F. Kennedy

Secrets of Success 20: SUPERSIZE YOUR MANIFESTATION MUSCLE WITH AN ATTITUDE OF GRATITUDE

Being aware of and knowing how to maintain a positive vibration is one of the most critical aspects of working with the **Secrets of Success.** The quickest and easiest way to do this is to develop and maintain an attitude of gratitude. When you follow the daily routine you start and finish your day focusing on the things that you are grateful for. By doing this you are creating the attitude of gratitude habit.

The continuous focus on setting daily goals that are linked to your vision, and the recognition of achieving them, allows you to recognise your part in manifesting each goal. Each and every time you achieve a goal it is essential that you declare to yourself and the Universe: 'Thank you, thank you, thank you.' I always add the word Universe to my expression of gratitude – 'Thank you Universe'. You may prefer to use a different form of gratitude. It really doesn't matter whom you thank as long as you actively express gratitude.

Your expression of gratitude raises your vibration. It affirms your belief that you are actively creating your future. It encourages you to continue with the process, creating a continuous virtuous cycle of success. I express gratitude for all of the achievements and manifestations that happen in my life. I also express gratitude when things don't turn out as I originally hoped. The reason I do this is that in order to protect and maintain my positive vibration I hold the belief that the Universe or my highest power knows best and if the thing I am asking for isn't showing up then I am either being protected from something or being guided to something better. I could also, of course, be sabotaging myself so I have to ensure that I have cleared any fears or negative self beliefs associated with the **ASK** in order to be in a place that allows me to truly trust the Universe to be doing what is right and best for me.

I have been challenged regarding this aspect of the process and I can't claim to understand every single event in my life. What I do know is that when I follow all of the principles and my vibration is high, I can manifest almost to order and often immediately.

When I first starting using the Drive-Thru Success process consciously I had so much success that I believed I could manifest like Samantha in *Bewitched*. All I had to do was wish and wriggle my nose and my every desire would appear. I was achieving so much success that I believed I was invincible.

I continue to be reminded by my oldest son of an amusing situation - at least it is amusing now, at the time it was nearly disastrous!

Gary had been set a school project for the Easter holidays. He had to research a city and write about it. I thought this would be a wonderful opportunity for he and I to have some mother-and-son time. So I suggested he pick Paris and we could go for a few days and he would learn all about the city, take his own photographs of the major landmarks and we would also go to Disneyland Paris for a day. This was all decided very quickly. I had a few days clear in my diary so I asked my husband to book us flights, which he duly did. He also tried to book us a hotel room in Disneyland but couldn't because they were fully booked.

He suggested that he could book me a hotel nearby, but I was so convinced that I could use Drive-Thru Success to manifest a hotel room that I said I would sort it out when we got there.

Gary wasn't so confident. He was 8 years old and kept asking me: 'What will we do if we can't get a hotel room in Disneyland mum?' My reply to him was: 'Oh Gary. You don't need to worry, the Universe will provide. Trust the Universe.'

Gary and I flew into Charles de Gaulle airport. We arrived at around 10pm at night. We got the train to Disneyland Paris and went straight to the Disneyland Hotel. I confidently asked the hotel receptionist for a twin room expecting her to hand me a key. By now it was nearly midnight. She asked me if I had a reservation, as every room was fully booked. I was totally shocked. This was not possible! The Universe was supposed to have sorted my room out. Gary was also confused: 'Mum, I thought the Universe was booking our room?'

I suggested to the receptionist that she must be mistaken and to check again. There had to be an empty room somewhere in the whole of Disneyland Paris! She checked again and sure enough she confirmed that due to a major conference being hosted in the resort, there indeed was no room anywhere! Not even a humble stable.

I had to admit defeat and started calling local hotels. We eventually got a room in a nearby non-Disney hotel. To this day I am curious as to why I didn't get that room. As it turned out the room we did get was so much cheaper that we were able to go to Disneyland Paris for two days instead of one. So even though we didn't get our room I still thanked the Universe for a great memorable trip to Paris.

Sadly, this experience to a very young Gary left him cynical for many years. More recently I have coached Gary and he now also uses the expression, 'Thank you Universe.'

What this experience has taught me is to combine using the **Drive-Thru Success** process alongside due diligence and common sense. I have learnt that trusting the Universe and embracing opportunities is wonderful, however I should also listen to my instincts and intuitions. Sometimes it's also wise to hit the pause button while I double-check that a course of action is the best course of action for me, is also wise. If the Universe comes up with the goods, great, however if I need to use more conventional methods, then I do.

I am grateful for knowing about the process. I am grateful for knowing about the **Secrets of Success** and I am grateful that I have experienced success and failure alike, as it has allowed me to consolidate my understanding of the principles. I don't really like to use the word failure, but I appreciate it has a powerful meaning for many people. Failing reminds me that my life is my life. I decide how I label my experiences and if I have failed then I get to decide if I want to develop a new or different strategy or choose a different path altogether. I understand that I have free choice and I am not defined by what happens in my life. I am defined by who I am, how I react to circumstances and how I behave in the face of adversity.

Although my life has had many challenges it has also had many blessings. I am surrounded by love. I am surrounded by abundance. I continue to approach each day with a curiosity as to what magical manifestation I can co-create with the Universe today. My life may not be perfect however my life is created by design - my design. I thank the Universe for each breath I take each day. I am happy to learn, grow and give service to each and every person who appears in my life with the purpose of sharing their love and their lessons. All I can say is thank you, thank you, thank you Universe.

Test Drive 20

Sometimes, before I pick up the pen, I don't know if I will be able to think of anything to be thankful for. Yet, never once have I left the page blank. At the very least, I can always thank the Universe for all of the basic things that I take for granted like sleeping in a warm, safe, comfortable home; having enough to eat and drink today; having people in my life that love and care about me; being able to get to sleep; and having the freedom and opportunity to choose what to do with my life.

There are millions of people around the world who don't have these things, and who are sitting somewhere at exactly the same time **ASK**ing for someone somewhere to help them have one or all of these things. I really owe it to them to appreciate what I have – something that I never used to do and that a lot of people never do despite living a wealthy, abundant life.

The habit of thinking about things to be grateful for is something that sticks with me throughout the day, and when I notice the things I have **ASK**ed for manifesting, it feels great to acknowledge that something wonderful just happened. I **ASK**ed for something and it came to me.

If you are like me, you will read many of these books and go on courses, and if it is one that speaks to you at the time, you will feel inspired and invigorated and raring to go. Yet it can be difficult to keep that momentum up. What is the difference between the people who say they are going to do the things, and the people who do the things? Of course it is practice.

There are things you need to do every day to put yourself in the right frame of mind. There are things you need to do every day to keep you on the road towards what it is you want to achieve. You have to do them whether you feel like it or not.

I have become aware that when I don't plan my days, write about the things I am grateful for, do Pranayama and meditate, I am less calm, less focused, and I feel like things are going wrong.

Having a purpose is a big key to feeling fulfilled. It doesn't really matter what

214

it is, but it needs to be something that inspires you, makes you feel good, makes time disappear when you do it, and it's a bonus if it betters the world in some way.

Like all of the other aspiring writers and creative people out there, I constantly doubt whether I am doing the right thing by spending my time on my creative projects, but did I ever question the purpose of the pictures I painted when I was a girl, or what the outcome would be of my singing a song, or listening to music? There's no end goal to the relationships I have. It's not like if I manage to create one perfect day filled with perfect feelings, my life goal will be complete and I'll disappear in a puff of smoke. I am learning to enjoy what I am doing as I do it it, and that is giving me a more fulfilling experience of life.

My goals are not always about achieving something finite – they can be about the way I want to experience my day. The daily routines outlined in this book have helped me to appreciate the way I am experiencing life and to give me the confidence and 'why not' attitude that allows me to go after my dreams. Sometimes I believe myself and sometimes I don't. The times when I don't are an experience too – I don't give myself too hard a time about them anymore.

Putting these principles into practice daily and sticking to them is difficult for everyone, but it is absolutely the difference between leaving the drive-thru with something you are unhappy with or nothing at all and picking up your order with a huge smile on your face, saying: 'Thank you, thank you, thank you.'

"Success is liking yourself, liking what you do, and liking how you do it."

Maya Angelou

Start Your Journey

I hope by now you have a real sense of how you can use the Drive-Thru Success principles in your life. I hope you have been able to put into practice the steps and secrets and are seeing the results. Please visit us at http://drive-thrusuccess.com/exercises/ where you can access all of the exercises as PDFs for your own use. Follow the instructions and we will send you an email with your password.

Join our @drivethrusuccess Facebook community and share your own ideas and experiences. We are always happy for people to contribute memes, experiences, and questions for the community to respond to. We will be 'going on the road', so if you want us to drive-thru your town, you can contact us through our website.

Engage in the manifestation process, every minute of every day:

The 3 simple steps in Drive-Thru Success

Step 1: ASK – place your order
Step 2: ACT – pay for your order
Step 3: ACTUALISE – pick up your order

Ensure your vibration is optimised at all times by embedding the **20 Secrets of Success** into the fabric of your life.

SOS 1: Being successful is easy
SOS 2: I am who I see myself to be
SOS 3: What you put your focus on is what you get
SOS 4: Be careful what you wish for, because you might just get it
SOS 5: If you want to predict your future, create it
SOS 6: Enjoy now, it is all you have
SOS 7: End with the start in mind, start with the end in heart
SOS 8: Would I rather be right than happy?
SOS 9: You can't please all of the people all of the time
SOS 10: There is no such thing as criticism, only feedback
SOS 11: Let it go!

SOS 12: You can monitor, manage, and maximise your energy

SOS 13: When I am being challenged, I must ask myself 'What do I need to learn now?'

SOS 14: Avoid people who have a problem for every solution

SOS 15: There is no such thing as a coincidence

SOS 16: Life is a series of choices

SOS 17: Choose to be a victor not a victim!

SOS 18: If you think you can or you think you can't you are right: Success at having things

SOS 19: Weebles wobble but they don't fall down

SOS 20: Supersize your manifesting muscle with an attitude of gratitude

Reviews

Thank you for joining us on our mission to create a better world by helping people to experience life in the best way possible.

If Drive-Thru Success has inspired you and you would like to pass that inspiration on, there is a way you can help us to share it with others.

Reviews are one of the most powerful ways you can help us to bring Drive-Thru Success to the attention of like-minded people all over the world. The more reviews we get, the more likely Amazon will recommend our book to other people.

Please take a few moments to share your honest thoughts about Drive-Thru Success (even a few words will make a difference).

www.amazon.co.uk/review/create-review/

With much love and gratitude

Jenny and Vhairi

Bibliography

Joyful Wisdom by Yongey Mingyur Rinpoche
The Power of Now by Eckhart Tolle
The Secret by Rhonda Byrne
Affirmations to Heal Your Life by Louise Hay
Grace by Christine McGrory
Think and Grow Rich by Napoleon Hill
Principles of Success by Jack Canfield

About the Authors

Jenny Copeland

Jenny, the author of Drive-Thru Success, is a passionate performance improvement coach. She has been delivering success to a variety of businesses and individuals for the past 30 years through her consultancy company, Secrets of Success. With an expert knowledge of coaching performance psychology, NLP and leadership, she designs and delivers development programmes, organisational solutions, and speeches for the NHS, private corporations, businesses, and individuals. She lives with her husband and three children and is always looking for her next challenge.

You can read more about Jenny at www.drive-thrusuccess.com and follow her on instragram @drivethrusuccess.

Vhairi Slaven

Vhairi is the co-writer and test-driver of Drive-Thru Success and the author of Miss Jane. She writes film reviews for www.moviescramble.co.uk, blogs on Facebook @VhairiSlavenwriter, and posts on Instagram @vhairislaven. She also teaches and practices yoga and works for the NHS in Communications. You can keep up with her work at www.vhairislaven.com.

Printed in Great Britain
by Amazon